Leonard Ravenhill
Why Revival Tarries

BY LEONARD RAVENHILL

Revival God's Way
Revival Praying
Why Revival Tarries

Leonard Ravenhill
Why Revival Tarries

BETHANYHOUSE
Minneapolis, Minnesota

Published by Bethany House Publishers
11400 Hampshire Avenue South
Bloomington, Minnesota 55438

Bethany House Publishers is a division of
Baker Publishing Group, Grand Rapids, Michigan.

Printed in the United States of America

ISBN 978-0-7642-2905-3

Library of Congress Cataloging-in-Publication Data

Ravenhill, Leonard.
    Why revival tarries / by Leonard Ravenhill.
        p.   cm.
    ISBN 0-7642-2905-2 (pbk.)
    1. Revivals. I. Title.

BV3790.R295   2004
269'.2—dc22   2004006164

To Martha, my gracious wife

LEONARD RAVENHILL was born in 1907 in the city of Leeds, in Yorkshire, England. After his conversion to Christ, he was trained for the ministry at Cliff College. It soon became evident that evangelism was his forte, and he engaged in it with both vigor and power. Eventually he became one of England's foremost outdoor evangelists. His meetings in the war years drew traffic-jamming crowds in Britain, and great numbers of his converts not only followed the Savior into the kingdom but also into the Christian ministry and the world's mission fields. He emigrated to the United States in midlife, where he continued his ministry. He and his wife, Martha, raised three sons. Ravenhill went home to be with the Lord in November 1994.

LEONARD RAVENHILL, MY FATHER

My mother was a singing mother. Every day as she carried me in her womb she sang and prayed for me. She and Granny, who lived next door to us, prayed together about the child that was to be born. An amazing thing happened two hours—not two months, not two weeks, not two days—after I was born. I was in a prayer meeting. My mother told me twenty years after, "When the midwife went out, I reached over the bed and laid my hands on you and just prayed, 'Lord, make this boy a preacher or don't let him live.'"

The above is a transcript of a forgotten tape that I was given only a matter of days ago in which my father recalls some of his early years. He was raised in a God-fearing home that believed in the power of prayer. His earliest recollection of school was that of being taught the Ten Commandments as a five-year-old as well as having to memorize and recite many of the Psalms. At the age of fourteen he was attending all-night prayer meetings—a passion he carried throughout his life.

He recalled: "They prayed with tears, they prayed with brokenness. They prayed for a lost world, then they began to pray for nations I knew little about. They had signs of Niagara Falls, but instead of water falling over, it was people dropping down."

My father's ministry started in England at the age of sixteen. His burden for the lost took him into the streets, where he began to preach to the local gypsy community—seventy-one years later he was on the streets of Glory.

My father was a powerfully anointed preacher who could bring down the convicting presence of God in a way that very few can. People would begin making their way to the altar even before any type of invitation was given, their hearts pierced by the Word of God. His preaching was superceded only by his passion for prayer. Like the apostle Paul, he carried "the daily pressure of concern for the church." Prayer was his life. Prior to his death in 1994 he told me he had received a number of requests from seminary students who wanted to come and see him for the sole purpose of having him lay his hands upon them in order to receive his "mantle." With his typical dry British humor, but at the same time deadly serious, he said, "Everyone wants to have my mantle but nobody wants my sackcloth and ashes." Sitting at his bedside only days after the stroke that was to take his life, I wrote these words:

Tribute to a Godly Man

I knew a man who gave his life
To see revival fire
He prayed by day, he prayed by night
to birth this one desire.

He had but one obsession
To see a glorious bride
Arrayed in spotless purity
Brought to her bridegroom's side.

His power while in the pulpit
Was matched by very few
And yet he loved the closet
There with the God he knew.

While others strove for man's applause
For fortune and for fame
He had but one ambition
To exalt his Master's name.

For eighty-seven years
He lived just for eternity
A man of faith and wisdom
And true humility.

He knew one day he'd have to stand
Before God's judgment seat
And so he ran to win the prize
His mission to complete.

The fortune that he left behind
Was not in stocks or gold
But lives transformed and challenged—
Their stories yet untold.

There is no greater privilege
Than this that I have had
Of knowing this great man of God
And having him as Dad.

—DAVID RAVENHILL,
AUTHOR AND ITINERANT TEACHER
LINDALE, TEXAS

CONTENTS

FOREWORD

Great industrial concerns have in their employ men who are needed only when there is a break-down somewhere. When something goes wrong with the machinery, these men spring into action to locate and remove the trouble and get the machinery rolling again.

For these men a smoothly operating system has no interest. They are specialists concerned with trouble and how to find and correct it.

In the kingdom of God things are not too different. God has always had His specialists whose chief concern has been the moral breakdown, the decline in the spiritual health of the nation or the church. Such men were Elijah, Jeremiah, Malachi, and others of their kind who appeared at critical moments in history to reprove, rebuke, and exhort in the name of God and righteousness.

A thousand or ten thousand ordinary priests or pastors or teachers could labor quietly almost unnoticed while the spiritual life of Israel or the church was normal. But let the people of God go astray from the paths of truth, and immediately the specialist appeared almost out of nowhere. His instinct for trouble brought him to the help of the Lord and of Israel.

Such a man was likely to be drastic, radical, possibly at times violent, and the curious crowd that gathered to watch him work soon branded him as extreme, fanatical, negative. And in a sense they were right. He was single-minded, severe, fearless, and these were the qualities the circumstances demanded. He shocked some, frightened others, and alienated not a few, but he knew who had called him and what he was sent to do. His ministry was geared to the emergency, and that fact marked him out as different, a man apart.

To such men as this the church owes a debt too heavy to pay. The curious thing is that she seldom tries to pay him while he lives, but the next generation builds his sepulcher and writes his biography, as if instinctively and awkwardly to discharge an obligation the previous generation to a large extent ignored.

Those who know Leonard Ravenhill will recognize in him the religious specialist, the man sent from God not to carry on the conventional work of the church, but to beard the priests of Baal on their own mountaintop, to shame the careless priest at the altar, to face the false prophet and warn the people who are being led astray by him.

Such a man as this is not an easy companion. The professional evangelist who leaves the wrought-up meeting as soon as it is over to hie him to the most expensive restaurant to feast and crack jokes with his retainers will find this man something of an embarrassment, for he cannot turn off the burden of the Holy Ghost as one would turn off a faucet. He insists upon being a Christian all the time, everywhere; and again, that marks him out as different.

Toward Leonard Ravenhill it is impossible to be neutral. His acquaintances are divided pretty neatly into two classes, those who love and admire him out of all proportion and those who hate him with perfect hatred. And what is true of the man is sure to be true of his books, of this book. The reader will either close its pages to seek a place of prayer or he will toss it away in anger, his heart closed to its warnings and appeals.

Not all books, not even all good books come as a voice from above, but I feel that this one does. It does because its author does, and the spirit of the author breathes through his book.

A. W. Tozer

PREFACE

Here is my simple offering of loaves and fishes—just plain diet, lacking the ice and spice of the wedding cake. Like a sailor I once saw pounding a soldier "because," said the sailor, "he insulted my mother," so my Lord is insulted and His Church slighted. And, believe me, under this double injury, I smart. The Church has many adversaries. Can my sword sleep, then, in my hand? Never!

I estimate that in the English edition alone, a million people read each issue of the "Herald of His Coming." Some of the chapters in this book are articles in old Heralds and have been read by millions. (I am neither ashamed nor proud of this.) There are a dozen other "Heralds" in Spanish, German, French, etc. Enough to say that through this paper, along with the "Alliance Witness" and other periodicals, God has seen fit to make non-academic essays a means of blessing to many. I pray that you gentle readers may be helped by them.

My sincere thanks to my esteemed friend and spiritual counselor, Dr. A. W. Tozer, for his kindness in writing the foreword. My unstinted praise to Mrs. Hines and her daughter, Ruth, for their fine work in typing and correcting the manuscripts. (All profits from this book go to overseas missions. May we live with eternity's values in view.)

Leonard Ravenhill

No erudition, no purity of diction, no width of mental outlook, no flowers of eloquence, no grace of person can atone for lack of fire. Prayer ascends by fire. Flame gives prayer access as well as wings, acceptance as well as energy. There is no incense without fire; no prayer without flame.

—**E. M. Bounds**

Bear up the hands that hang down, by faith and prayer; support the tottering knees. Have you any days of fasting and prayer? Storm the throne of grace and persevere therein, and mercy will come down.

—**John Wesley**

Before the great revival in Gallneukirchen broke out, Martin Boos spent hours and days and often nights in lonely agonies of intercession. Afterwards, when he preached, his words were as flame, and the hearts of the people as grass.

—**D. M. McIntyre, D.D.**

How many Christians there are who cannot pray, and who seek by effort, resolve, joining prayer circles, etc., to cultivate in themselves the "holy art of intercession," and all to no purpose. Here for them and for all is the only secret of a real prayer life—"Be filled with the Spirit," who is "the Spirit of grace and supplication."

—**Rev. J. Stuart Holden**

With All Thy Getting, Get Unction

The Cinderella of the church of today is the prayer meeting. This handmaid of the Lord is unloved and unwooed because she is not dripping with the pearls of intellectualism, nor glamorous with the silks of philosophy; neither is she enchanting with the tiara of psychology. She wears the homespuns of sincerity and humility and so is not afraid to kneel!

The offense of prayer is that it does not essentially tie in to mental efficiency. (That is not to say that prayer is a partner to mental sloth; in these days efficiency is at a premium.) Prayer is conditioned by one thing alone and that is spirituality. One does not need to be spiritual to preach, that is, to make and deliver sermons of homiletical perfection and exegetical exactitude. By a combination of memory, knowledge, ambition, personality, plus well-lined bookshelves, self-confidence, and a sense of having arrived—brother, the pulpit is yours almost anywhere these days. Preaching of the type mentioned affects men; prayer affects God. Preaching affects time; prayer affects eternity. The pulpit can be a shopwindow to display our talents; the closet speaks death to display.

The tragedy of this late hour is that we have too many *dead* men in the pulpits giving out too many *dead* sermons to too many *dead* people. Oh! the horror of it. There is a strange thing that I have seen "under the sun," even in the fundamentalist circles; it is preaching without unction. What is unction? I hardly know. But I know what it is not (or at least I know when it is not upon my own soul). Preaching without unction kills instead of giving life. The unctionless preacher is a savor of death unto death. The Word does not live unless the unction is upon the preacher. *Preacher, with all thy getting—get unction.*

Brethren, we could well manage to be half as intellectual (of the modern pseudo kind) if we were twice as spiritual. Preaching is a spiritual business. A sermon born in the head reaches the head; a sermon born in the heart reaches the heart. Under God, a spiritual preacher will produce spiritually minded people. Unction is not a gentle dove beating her wings against the bars outside of the preacher's soul; rather, she must be pursued and won. Unction cannot be learned, only earned—by prayer. Unction is God's knighthood for the soldier-preacher who has wrestled in prayer and gained the victory. Victory is not won in the pulpit by firing intellectual bullets or wisecracks, but in the prayer closet; it is won or lost before the preacher's foot enters the pulpit. Unction is like dynamite. Unction comes not by the medium of the bishop's hands, neither does it mildew when the preacher is cast into prison. Unction will pierce and percolate; it will sweeten and soften. When the hammer of logic and the fire of human zeal fail to open the stony heart, unction will succeed.

What a fever of church building there is just now! Yet

without unctionized preachers, these altars will never see anxious penitents. Suppose that we saw fishing boats, with the latest in radar equipment and fishing gear, launched month after month and put out to sea only to return without a catch—what excuse would we take for this barrenness? Yet thousands of churches see empty altars week after week and year after year, and cover this sterile situation by misapplying the Scripture, "My word . . . shall not return unto me void." (Incidentally, this seems to be one of the very few texts that the dispensationalists forgot to tell us was written to the Jews!)

The ugly fact is that altar fires are either out or burning very low. The prayer meeting is dead or dying. By our attitude to prayer we tell God that what was begun in the Spirit we can finish in the flesh. What church ever asks its candidating ministers what time they spend in prayer? Yet ministers who do not spend two hours a day in prayer are not worth a dime a dozen, degrees or no degrees.

The church today is standing on the sidewalk, watching with fever and frustration, while the sin-dominated evil geniuses of Moscow strut the middle of the road, breathing out threatenings against "whatsoever things are lovely and of good report." Behind, follows the purple pageantry of papal Rome. Moreover, the devil has substituted reincarnation for regeneration, familiar spirits for the Holy Spirit, Christian Science for divine healing, the Antichrist for the true Christ, and the Church of Rome for the true Church.

Against these twin evils of Communism and Romanism, what has the Church to offer? Where is the supernatural? Both in the pulpit and in the press, somnolence seems to have overtaken religious controversy of late. Even Rome does not call us Protestants any more; we have just the juiceless name of non-Catholics! Significant, isn't it? Hell has no fury like that of this "Mother of Harlots" *when she is stirred.* But who now "earnestly contends for the faith once delivered to the saints"? Where are our unctionized pulpit crusaders? Preachers who should be fishing for men are now too often fishing for compliments from men. Preachers used to sow seed; now they string intellectual pearls. (Imagine a field sown with pearls!)

Away with this palsied, powerless preaching which is unmoving because it was born in a tomb instead of a womb, and nourished in a fireless, prayerless soul. We may preach and perish, but we cannot pray and perish. If God called us to the ministry, then, dear brethren, I contend that we should get unctionized. *With all thy getting—get unction,* lest barren altars be the badge of our unctionless intellectualism.

Our praying, however, needs to be pressed and pursued with an energy that never tires, a persistency which will not be denied, and a courage which never fails.

—E. M. BOUNDS

But ye, beloved, building up yourselves on your most holy faith, PRAYING IN THE HOLY GHOST.

—JUDE

O that we were more deeply moved by the languishing state of Christ's cause upon the earth today, by the inroads of the enemy and the awful desolation he has wrought in Zion. Alas that a spirit of indifference, or at least of fatalistic stoicism, is freezing so many of us.

—A. W. PINK

Prayer was pre-eminently the business of his life.

—BIOGRAPHER OF EDWIN PAYSON

Whole days and WEEKS have I spent prostrate on the ground in silent or vocal prayer.

—GEORGE WHITEFIELD

All decays begin in the closet; no heart thrives without much secret converse with God, and nothing will make amends for the want of it.

—BERRIDGE

It seemed to me as if he had gone straight into heaven, and lost himself in God; but often when he had done praying he was as white as the wall.

—A FRIEND'S COMMENT AFTER MEETING TERSTEEGEN AT KRONENBERG

CHAPTER TWO

Prayer Grasps Eternity

REALLY? BIBLICAL?

No man is greater than his prayer life. The pastor who is not praying is playing; the people who are not praying are straying. The pulpit can be a shopwindow to display one's talents; the prayer closet allows no showing off.

Poverty-stricken as the Church is today in many things, she is most stricken here, in the place of prayer. We have many organizers, but few agonizers; many players and payers, few pray-ers; many singers, few clingers; lots of pastors, few wrestlers; many fears, few tears; much fashion, little passion; many interferers, few intercessors; many writers, but few fighters. Failing here, we fail everywhere.

The two prerequisites to successful Christian living are vision and passion, both of which are born in and maintained by prayer. The ministry of preaching is open to few; the ministry of prayer—the highest ministry of all human offices—is open to all. Spiritual adolescents say, "I'll not go tonight, it's only the prayer meeting." It may be that Satan has little cause to fear most preaching. Yet past experiences sting him to rally all his infernal army to fight against God's people praying. Modern Christians know little of "binding and loosing," though the onus is on us—"Whatsoever *ye* shall bind. . . ." Have you done any of this lately? God is not

I'D SAY NOT ONLY PRAYER THOUGH

prodigal with His power; but to be much for God, we must be much with God.

This world hits the trail for hell with a speed that makes our fastest plane look like a tortoise; yet alas, few of us can remember the last time we missed our bed for a night of waiting upon God for a world-shaking revival. Our compassions are not moved. We mistake the scaffolding for the building. Present-day preaching, with its pale interpretation of divine truths, causes us to mistake action for unction, commotion for creation, and rattles for revivals.

The secret of praying is praying in secret. A sinning man will stop praying, and a praying man will stop sinning. We are beggared and bankrupt, but not broken, nor even bent.

Prayer is profoundly simple and simply profound. "Prayer is the simplest form of speech that infant lips can try," and yet so sublime that it outranges all speech and exhausts man's vocabulary. A Niagara of burning words does not mean that God is either impressed or moved. One of the most profound of Old Testament intercessors had no language—"Her lips moved, *but her voice was not heard.*" No linguist here! There *are* "groanings which cannot be uttered."

Are we so substandard to New Testament Christianity that we know not the historical faith of our fathers (with its implications and operations), but only the hysterical faith of our fellows? Prayer is to the believer what capital is to the business man.

Can any deny that in the modern church setup the main cause of anxiety is money? Yet that which tries the modern churches the most, troubled the New Testament Church the least. Our accent is on paying, theirs was on praying. When we have paid, the place is taken; when they had prayed, the place was shaken!

In the matter of New Testament, Spirit-inspired, hell-shaking, world-breaking prayer, never has so much been left by so many to so few.

For this kind of prayer there is no substitute. We do it—or die!

A religion of mere emotion and sensationalism is the most terrible of all curses that can come upon any people. The absence of reality is sad enough, but the aggravation of pretence is a deadly sin.

—SAMUEL CHADWICK

It is well to get rid of the idea that faith is a matter of spiritual heroism only for a few select spirits. There are heroes of faith, but faith is not only for heroes. It is a matter of spiritual manhood. It is a matter of maturity.

—P. T. FORSYTH

When God intends great mercy for His people, the first thing He does is set them a-praying.

—MATTHEW HENRY

Truth without enthusiasm, morality without emotion, ritual without soul, are things Christ unsparingly condemned. Destitute of fire, they are nothing more than a godless philosophy, an ethical system, and a superstition.

—SAMUEL CHADWICK

The call of the Cross, therefore, is to enter into this passion of Christ. We must have upon us the print of the nails.

—GORDON WATT

My need and Thy great fulness meet,
And I have all in Thee.

—UNKNOWN

I have seen faces upon which the Dove sat visibly brooding.

—CHARLES LAMB ON THE
QUAKERS

Fervent in Spirit, serving the Lord.

—PAUL

CHAPTER THREE

A Call for Unction in the Pulpit—Action in the Pew!

When a man who has crept along for years in conventional Christianity suddenly zooms into spiritual alertness, becomes aggressive in the battle of the Lord, and has a quenchless zeal for the lost, there is a reason for it. (But we are so subnormal these days that the normal New Testament experience seems abnormal.) The secret of this "jet-propelled fellow" we have just mentioned is that somewhere *he has had Jacob-like wrestlings with God and has come out stripped, but also "strengthened by the Holy Ghost!"*

There are two indispensable factors to successful Christian living. They are *vision* and *passion*. Men battle mountainous seas of human. carnal criticism and storm the flinty heights of devilish opposition to plant the cross of Christ amidst the habitations of cruelty. Why? Because they have caught a vision and contracted a passion.

Someone now warns us lest we become so heavenly minded that we are of no earthly use. Brother, this generation of believers is not, by and large, suffering from such a complex! The brutal, soul-shaking truth is that we are so earthly minded we are of no heavenly use.

Friend, if you were as good at soul-cultivation as you are in developing your business, you would be a menace to the devil; but if you were as poor in business matters as you are in soul, you would be begging for bread.

George Deakin drummed into my mind many years ago this fine bit of spiritual reasoning: A vision without a task makes a visionary; a task without a vision is drudgery; a vision with a task makes a missionary. Well said! Isaiah had a vision *when Uzziah died!* Maybe there is some person in your way blotting out the full vision of the Lord. Spiritual expansion is expensive and at times excruciating. Are you prepared for vision at this top-price demand—the loss of a friend or a career? There are no reduced rates for revolution of soul. If you only want to be saved, sanctified, and satisfied, then the Lord's battle hath no need of thee.

Isaiah had a vision in three dimensions. Note verses one to nine in the sixth chapter of Isaiah. Verse five, *WOE,* a word of *confession;* verse seven, *LO,* a word of *cleansing;* verse nine, *GO,* a word of *commission.*

It was an *upward* vision—he saw the Lord; an *inward* vision—he saw himself, and an *outward* vision—he saw the world.

It was a vision of *height*—he saw the Lord high and lifted up. A vision of *depth*—he saw the recesses of his own heart. And a vision of *breadth*—he saw the world.

A vision of *holiness.* Oh, beloved! How this generation of believers needs the vision of God in all His holiness! A vision of *hellishness*—"I am undone. . . . unclean!" and a vision of *hopelessness*—implied by the words "Who will go for us?"

In this hour—when the average church knows more

about promotion than prayer, has forgotten consecration by fostering competition, and has substituted propaganda for propagation—this threefold vision is imperative.

"Where there is no vision the *people* perish." Where there is no passion the *church* perishes, even though it be full to the doors.

A world-famed preacher, who has been mightily used of God in the past few years in real revival (distinct and very different from mass evangelism), told the writer that he had a similar threefold vision. I can still see the solemn dread on that face as he spoke of hardly knowing whether he was having a dream or seeing a vision, not knowing whether he was in the body or transported; yet he could see a multitude that no man could number in a large abyss—surrounded by fire—locked in the "madhouse of the universe," *HELL*. This preacher has never been the same since. How could he be?

Could God entrust us with such a heartbreaking revelation? Have we graduated in the secret place of prayer and in the school of suffering so that our spirits are tempered to bear such a soul-sickening sight? Blessed is the man to whom the Lord can impart such a vision!

No man lives beyond his vision. Heavy-minded theologians cannot break open the iron curtains of superstition and darkness behind which, for millenniums, millions have perished. Only men with less breadth of intellect, maybe, but with more depth of vision can do that.

To be spiritually minded is joy and peace. Yet to be statistically minded in addition can be very disturbing. Read this and weep:

JAPAN—The government there states that the population has passed the eighty-seven million mark. The nation is growing at the rate of one million one hundred thousand a year! This means that the non-Christian population of Japan has increased by five million in the past five years. Put this well up on your prayer list.

KOREA—Here are nine million people mostly refugees, homeless and almost foodless.

INDIA—Millions sit in darkness and in the shadow of death.

MIDDLE EAST—Here are a million Arab refugees.

EUROPE—She has eleven million "displaced persons." What a heartache for them!

CHINA—A third of a million escapees are from communist China, living in squatters' huts in Hong Kong.

To add to your burden and mine, there are fifteen million Jews; three hundred and fifteen million Muslims; one hundred and seventy million Buddhists; three hundred and fifty million Confucianists and Taoists; two hundred and fifty-five million Hindus; ninety million Shintoists; and millions of others, for whom Christ died and who are mainly unreached with the blessed Gospel. Even church-conscious America has twenty-seven million youth under twenty-one years of age who receive no Christian training, and ten thousand villages that do not have a church building. Almost a million persons in the world die each week without Christ. *Is this nothing to you?*

This sin-swamped situation calls for unction in the pulpit and action in the pew! Synthetic religion must go. The Amen Corner has passed away with the model-T Ford; the camp-meeting glory has vanished; zeal for street meetings has evaporated.

Maybe—who knows?—God is more wroth with America and England than He is with Russia! Is that shocking? Then consider soberly that millions in Russia have never heard a gospel message, never had a Bible, and never listened to a spiritual broadcast. They would go to a church if they could. ˉ ๆ๙๙

The repeated prayer that the sinner might have a vision of hell may be entirely wrong. On the contrary, he probably needs a vision of Calvary, with a suffering Saviour pleading ~ ฿ฃ๙ with him to repent; for after Calvary, why should he die? William Booth of the Salvation Army is quoted as saying that if he could do it, he would have finalized the training of his soldiers with twenty-four hours hanging over hell, to see its eternal torment. Fundamentalism needs this awe-striking vision again. The gusty, grandiloquent evangelist needs it most!

Charlie Peace was a criminal. Laws of God or man curbed him not. Finally the law caught up with him, and he was condemned to death. On the fatal morning in Armley Jail, Leeds, England, he was taken on the death-walk. Before him went the prison chaplain, routinely and sleepily reading some Bible verses. The criminal touched the preacher and asked what he was reading. "The Consolations of Religion," was the reply. Charlie Peace was shocked at the way he professionally read about hell. Could a man be so unmoved under the very shadow of the scaffold as to lead a fellow-human there and yet, dry-eyed, read of a pit that has no bottom into which this fellow must fall? Could this preacher believe the words that there is an eternal fire that never consumes its victims, and yet slide over the phrase without a tremor? Is a man human at all who can say with no tears, "You will be eternally dying and yet never know the relief that death brings"? All this was too much for Charlie Peace. So he preached. Listen to his on-the-eve-of-hell sermon.

"Sir," addressing the preacher, "if I believed what you and the church of God *say* that you believe, even if England were covered with broken glass from coast to coast, I would walk over it, if need be, on hands and knees and think it worthwhile living, just to save one soul from an eternal hell like that!"

FALSE

My reader, because the Church has lost Holy Ghost fire, men go to hell-fire! We need a vision of a holy God. God is essentially holy. The cherubim and seraphim were not crying, "Omnipotent! Omnipotent is the Lord!" nor "Omnipresent! and Omniscient! is the Lord," but "Holy! Holy Holy!" This vast Hebrew concept needs to penetrate our souls again. If I make my bed in hell, if I take the wings of the morning—yet He is there. God compasses us in time; God, the inescapable God, awaits us in eternity. We had better be at peace with Him *here,* and be in the center of His will *now!*

To wait tremblingly before this thrice-holy One before we leave home for the day's work would be a mighty soul-stimulant. He who fears God fears no man. He who kneels before God will stand in any situation. A daily glimpse at the Holy One would find us subdued by His omnipresence, staggered by His omnipotence, silenced by His omniscience, and solemnized by His holiness. *His* holiness would become *our* holiness. Holiness-teaching contradicted by unholy living is the bane of this hour! "A holy minister is an awful weapon in the hands of God." So said Robert Murray McCheyne.

Before the experiences of the sixth chapter, Isaiah has a lot of woes for a lot of people. Now he sees himself and cries, "Woe is *me!*" "It's *me,* it's *me,* O Lord, standing in the need of prayer!" How true! Are there chambers of the mind with unclean pictures hanging in them? Have we skeletons in the cupboards of our hearts? Can the Holy Ghost be invited to take us by the hand down the corridors of our souls? Are there not secret springs, and secret motives that control, and secret chambers where polluted things hold empire over the soul? There are three persons living in each of us: the one we think we are, the one other people think we are, and the one God *knows* we are.

Unless we are desperate to get into real victory, we are so easy on ourselves and so hard on others! Self loves self, though it was said of Gerard Majella that by grace "he loved all men except Gerard Majella." Great possibility! But too often we hide ourselves from ourselves lest the sight of ourselves should sicken ourselves. Let us invite the searching eye of God to locate this corrupted, spotted, stinking Self in us. Let it be torn from us and "crucified with Him, (so) that henceforth we no longer serve sin" (Rom. 6:6).

It will not do to call sin by some other name, saying, "The other fellow has a devilish temper; mine is just righteous indignation! She is touchy; my irritability is just 'a case of nerves.' He is covetous; I am expanding my business. He is stubborn; I have convictions. She is proud; I have superior tastes." There is a cover-up for anything if you want it that way.

But the Spirit will neither spare us nor cheat us if we will expose ourselves to His infallible scrutiny. Jesus said unto [the blind man], "What wilt thou that I should do unto thee? [He] said unto him, Lord, that I might receive my sight" (Mark 10:51). Let us, too, pray for sight—upward, inward, and outward! Then like Isaiah, as we look *upward,* we will see the Lord in all His holiness; as we look *inward,* we will see ourselves and our need for cleansing and power; and as we look *outward,* we will see a world that is perishing and in need of a Saviour! "Search *me, O* God, and know *my* heart: try *me,* and know *my* thoughts: and see if there be any wicked way in *me,* and lead *me* in the way everlasting" (Psalm 139:23-24). Then only will there be *unction in the pulpit and action in the pew!*

Do not we rest in our day too much on the arm of flesh?
Cannot the same wonders be done now as of old? Do not
the eyes of the Lord still run to and fro throughout the
whole earth to show Himself strong on behalf of those
who put their trust in Him? Oh, that God would give me
more practical faith in Him! Where is now the Lord God
of Elijah? He is waiting for Elijah to call on Him.

—James Gilmour of Mongolia

We know the utility of prayer from the efforts of the
wicked spirits to distract us during the divine office;
and we experience the fruit of prayer in the defeat
of our enemies.

—John Climacus

When we go to God by prayer,
the devil knows we go to fetch strength against him,
and therefore he opposeth us all he can.

—R. Sibbes

I sought for a man.

—Ezekiel 22:30

Elias was a man.

—James 5:17

CHAPTER FOUR

Where Are the Elijahs of God?

To the question, "Where is the Lord God of Elijah?" we answer, "Where He has always been—on the throne!" But where are the Elijahs of God? We know Elijah was "a man of like passions as we are," but alas! we are not men of like prayer as he was! One praying man stands as a majority with God! Today God is bypassing men—not because they are too ignorant, but because they are too self-sufficient. Brethren, our abilities are our handicaps, and our talents our stumbling blocks! —TO US

Out of obscurity, Elijah came on to the Old Testament stage, a full-grown man. Queen Jezebel, that daughter of hell, had routed the priests of God and replaced them with groves to false deities. Darkness covered the land and gross darkness the people, and they were drinking iniquity like water. Every day the land, fouled with heathen temples and idolatrous rites, saw smoke curling from a thousand cruel altars.

All this was among a people who claimed Abraham as their father, and whose forebears had cried unto the Lord in their trouble and He had delivered them out of all their distresses. How the God of Glory had departed! the salt had lost its savour! the gold had become dim! But out of this measureless backsliding, God raised up a man—not a committee, not a sect, not an angel—but a *MAN*, and a man of like passions as we are! God *"sought for a man,"* not to preach, but *"to stand in the gap."* As Abraham, so now Elijah *"stood before the Lord."* Therefore the blessed Holy Spirit could write the life of Elijah in two words: *"He prayed."* No man can do more than that for God or for men. If the Church today had as many agonizers as she has advisers, we would have a revival in a year!

Such praying men are always our national benefactors. Elijah was such. He had heard a voice, seen a vision, tasted a power, measured an enemy, and, with God as partner, wrought a victory. The tears he shed, the soul agonies he endured, the groans he uttered, are all recorded in the book of the chronicles of the things of God. At last Elijah emerged to prophesy with divine infallibility. He knew the mind of God. Therefore he—one man—strangled a nation and altered the course of nature. This "crag of a man" stood as majestic and immovable as the mountains of Gilead, as he shut up the heavens with a word. By the key of faith, which fits every lock, Elijah locked heaven, pocketed the key, and made Ahab tremble. Though it is wonderful indeed when God lays hold of a man, earth can know one greater wonder—when a man lays hold of God. Let a man of God "in the Spirit" *groan,* and God will cry out, *"Let me alone."* We would like Elijah's accomplishments, but not his banishments!

Brethren, if we will do God's work in God's way at God's time with God's power, we shall have God's blessing and the devil's curses. When God opens the windows of heaven to bless us, the devil will open the door of hell to blast us. God's

smile means the devil's frown! Mere preachers may help anybody and hurt nobody; but prophets will stir everybody and
madden somebody. The preacher may go *with* the crowd;
the prophet goes *against* it. A man freed, fired, and filled
with God will be branded unpatriotic because he speaks
against his nation's sins; unkind because his tongue is a two-
edged sword; unbalanced because the weight of preaching
opinion is against him. The preacher will be heralded; the
prophet hounded.

Ah! brother preachers, we love the old saints, missionaries, martyrs, reformers: our Luthers, Bunyans, Wesleys,
Asburys, etc. We will write their biographies, reverence their
memories, frame their epitaphs, and build their cenotaphs.[7]
We will do anything except imitate them. We cherish the last
drop of their blood, but watch the first drop of our own!

John the Baptist did well to evade prison for six months.
He and Elijah would not last six weeks in the streets of a
modern city. They would be cast into a prison or mental
home for judging sin and not muting their message.

Evangelists today are wide-eyed to the might of Communism, but tight-lipped at the menace of Romanism. America would shake from coast to coast in twenty-four hours if
some preacher, anointed with the Holy Ghost, gave the
Roman Catholic Church a broadside! In England we are
worse. We stir national interest against the cruel, half-
civilized Mau Mau (wicked enough!), but powwow with, and
pander to, the Roman Catholic Church! These priests who
dope men's souls, these idolatrous "masses," these Calvary-
eclipsing prayers to Mary, these miserable millions cheated
in life and in death by the greatest forgery Lucifer ever
made—all these do not seem to stir us to tearful interces-
sions and godly jealousy, as identical circumstances stirred
Elijah. The enemy has come in like a flood. Is there no Spirit-

filled messenger today, armed with all the panoply of God, to lift up a standard against him? One place alone will keep the heart in passion and the eyes in vision—the place of prayer. This man Elijah, with a volcano for a heart, and a thunderstorm for a voice, came to the Kingdom for such a time as this.

The difficulties to world evangelism are legion. But difficulties give way to determined men.

> "Got any rivers you think are uncrossable?
> Got any mountains you can't tunnel through?
> God specializes in things thought impossible,
> And He can do what no other pow'r can do."

The price is high. God does not want partnership with us, but ownership of us.

Elijah lived with God. He thought about the nation's sin *like God;* he grieved over sin *like God;* he spoke against sin *like God.* He was all passion in his prayers and passionate in his denunciation of evil in the land. He had no smooth preaching. Passion fired his preaching, and his words were on the hearts of men as molten metal on their flesh.

But "the steps of a good man are ordered by the Lord" (Psalm 37:23). The Lord said to Elijah, "Hide thyself," and again, "Show thyself." It would be wrong to hide when we should be rebuking kings for His sake; it would be wrong to preach if the Spirit is calling us to wait upon the Lord. We must learn with David, "My soul, wait thou only upon God" (Psalm 62:5). Who of us dares to invite the Lord to cut out all our props? God's ways are not our ways. His ways are "past finding out," but He reveals them unto us by His Spirit. God ordered Elijah to Cherith, then to Zarephath—to lodge at a swank hotel? No! No! This prophet of God, this preacher of righteousness, was commanded by the Lord to stay at the home of an impoverished widow!

Later, Elijah's prayer at Carmel was a masterpiece of concise praying. *"Hear me, O Lord, hear me, that this people may know that thou art the Lord God, and that thou hast turned their heart back again"* (I Kings 18:37). E. M. Bounds is right in saying that short, powerful public prayers are the outcome of long secret intercession. Elijah prayed, not for the destruction of the idolatrous priests, nor for thunderbolts from heaven to consume rebellious Israel, but that the glory of God and the power of God might be revealed.

We try to help God out of difficulties. Remember how Abraham tried to do this, and to this day the earth is cursed with his folly because of Ishmael. On the other hand, Elijah made it as difficult as he could for the Lord. He wanted fire, but yet he soaked the sacrifice with water! God loves such holy boldness in our prayers. "Ask of me, and I shall give thee the heathen for thine inheritance, and the uttermost parts of the earth for thy possession" (Psalm 2:8).

Oh! my ministering brethren! Much of our praying is but giving God advice! Our praying is discolored with ambition, either for ourselves or for our denomination. Perish the thought! Our goal must be God alone. It is His honor that is sullied, His blessed Son who is ignored, His laws broken, His name profaned, His Book forgotten, His house made a circus of social efforts.

Does God ever need more patience with His people than when they are "praying"? We tell Him what to do and how to do it. We pass judgments and make appreciations in our prayers. In short, we do everything except pray. No Bible School can teach us this art. What Bible School has "Prayer" on its curriculum? The most important thing a man can study is the prayer part of the Book. But where is this taught? Let us strip off the last bandage and declare that many of our presidents and teachers do not pray, shed no tears, know no travail. Can they teach what they do not know?

The man who can get believers to praying would, under God, usher in the greatest revival that the world has ever known. There is *no* fault in God. He is able. God *"is able to do . . . according to the power that worketh in us."* God's problem today is not Communism, nor yet Romanism, nor Liberalism, nor Modernism. God's problem is—dead fundamentalism!

Revival and evangelism, although closely linked, are not to be confounded. Revival is an experience in the Church; evangelism is an expression of the Church.

—**PAUL S. REES**

God never intended His Church to be a refrigerator in which to preserve perishable piety. He intended it to be an incubator in which to hatch out converts.

—**F. LINCICOME**

Lord, is it I?

—**THE DISCIPLES**

Got any rivers you think are uncrossable?
Got any mountains you can't tunnel through?
God specializes in things thought impossible,
And He can do what no other pow'r can do.

God helps us seek popularity where it counts—
at the court of God!

—**ZEPP**

CHAPTER FIVE

Revival in a Bone Yard

The hand of the Lord was upon me, and carried me out in the Spirit of the Lord, and set me down in the midst of the valley which was full of bones . . . and, behold, there were very many . . . and lo, they were dry . . . And He said unto me . . . Prophesy upon these bones, and say unto them, O ye dry bones, hear the word of the Lord . . . So I prophesied as I was commanded . . . and the breath came into them, and they lived and stood upon their feet, an exceeding great army" (Ezekiel 37).

Does history, sacred or profane, offer a more ridiculous picture than this? Here is hopelessness incarnate. Who ever had such a dumb audience? Preachers deal with possibilities, prophets with impossibilities. Isaiah had seen this nation full of wounds and putrefying sores; but disease had galloped on to death, death to disintegration, and now these disjointed bones spell out despair. Written over the whole situation in large capitals is *I-M-P-O-S-S-I-B-I-L-I-T-Y.* Now obviously no faith is required to do *the possible;* actually only a morsel of this atom-powered stuff is needed to do *the impossible,* for a piece as large as a mustard seed will do more than we have ever dreamed of. Again and again God asks men to do not what they can, but what they can't. To prove that no sleight of hand does it but that they link their impotence to His omnipotence, the word *impossible* is dropped from their vocabularies.

Prophets are lone men: they walk alone, pray alone, and God makes them alone. For them there is no mold; their patent rights are with God, for the principle of divine selection is "past finding out." But let no man despair; let none of us say, however we may have been or have not been used, that we are too old. Moses was eighty when he took command of an enslaved and broken people. After George Mueller was seventy, he went around the world several times and, without the aid of radio, preached to millions of people.

As for Ezekiel, he called no committee and sent out no prayer letter; he solicited no funds and loathed publicity. But this situation was a matter of Life and Death. (So is evangelism today—therefore, let every preacher beware lest his "theological-juggling" act send his hearer home saying, "He is a clever fellow!" and yet leave him in complete spiritual darkness.) To this mountain of bones, then, Ezekiel was asked to say, *"Be thou removed!"* So he said and so it was. Here was a curse—had he a cure? Here was death—could he bring life? This was no pretty declaration of doctrine. Dear believers, listen. The world is not waiting for a new definition of the Gospel, but for a new demonstration of the power of the Gospel. In these days of acute political helplessness, moral lawlessness, and spiritual helplessness, where are the men not of doctrine, but of faith? No faith is required to curse the darkness or give staggering statistical evidence that the dikes are down and a tidal wave of hellish impurity has submerged this generation. Doctrine?—we have enough and to spare, while a sick, sad, sin-sodden, sex-soaked world perishes with hunger.

At this grim hour, the world sleeps in the darkness, and the Church sleeps in the light; so Christ is "wounded in the house of His friends." The limping Church militant is derisively called the Church impotent. Yearly we use mountains of paper and rivers of ink reprinting dead men's brains, while the living Holy Ghost is seeking for men to trample underfoot their own learning, deflate their inflated ego, and confess that with all their seeing they are blind. Such men, at the price of brokenness and strong crying and tears, seek that they may be anointed with divine eyesalve, bought at the price of honest acknowledgment of poverty of soul. Years ago a minister put this sign outside of his church, "This church will have either a revival or a funeral!" With such despair God is well pleased, though hell is despondent. Madness, you say? Exactly! A sober church never does any good. At this hour we need men drunk with the Holy Ghost. Has God excelled Himself? Were Wesley, Whitefield, Finney, Hudson Taylor special editions of ministers? Never! If I read the Book of Acts aright, they were just the norm.

The atom bomb seems to have disturbed everything— except the Church. By overstating the sovereignty of God and blundering on in an atmosphere of stagnant dispensationalism, we safeguard our spiritual bankruptcy. All the while hell fills. With Communism in the world, Modernism in the churches, and Moderatism crippling the fundamentalist groups, will the Lord look in vain for a man to stand in the gap, as Ezekiel did? My preacher brethren, these days we are more fond of travelling than travailing, hence—no births. God send us, and that right early, a prophet out of step with a church which is out of joint.

The hour is too late for another denomination to be born.

REALLY?

Right now, God is preparing His Elijahs for the last great earthly offensive against militant godlessness (whether political or wearing a mask of religion). The last great outpouring of revival, Holy Ghost born and operated, will be new wine bursting the skins of dried-up sectarianism. Hallelujah!

Note that Ezekiel was *Spirit-led*. As a man, he must have shuddered at the appalling sight of mountains of dry human bones. But pivoted on Ezekiel's faith was the destiny of thousands if not millions—pivoted on faith, mark you, not prayer. Many pray, but few have faith. What holy tremors must have rushed through his soul at this sight! Only heaven and hell were spectators. Surely if Ezekiel were living today, he would have had a press photograph of this! Next, with a love of statistics, he would have *counted* the bones; when things had begun to move, he certainly would have called others to see him operate (lest men fail to give him the right ranking with national evangelists!). Not so Ezekiel. Listen to this: *"I prophesied as I was commanded"* (there is the crux of the matter—he was a fool for God); *"O ye dry bones, hear the word of the Lord."* Madness? Yes, insanity—of virgin purity! He said to the bones, *"Hear!"* though they had no ears! Ezekiel did as he was told. To save our faces, we of course modify God's commands, and so lose our faces. But Ezekiel obeyed; and God, as always, operated: *"there was a great noise."* Well—*that* would suit us. But Ezekiel did not mistake commotion for creation, nor action for unction, nor rattle for revival.

With only *one* breath from His omnipotent lips, God *could* have raised this heap to life, but no—there were to be *many* operations. First, *"Bones came together, bone to his bone."* (No mountain of bones now.) Such phenomena would almost put us into hysterics; not so Ezekiel. But what good are skeletons? Can these fight the battles of the Lord? At this

stage would they bring honor to His Name? Too often today
blind guides count "skeletons" who come to the altars—
moved certainly, but not yet born. At their few, hot tears we
exhort, "Believe this promise." But as yet they have no life.
Even so, flesh must come upon the skeletons; then skin must
cover the flesh. And the result is that we have a valley full
of—corpses! Any good to God? Not yet. They have eyes but
cannot see, hands but cannot fight, feet but cannot walk. So
are those who are seeking—until this last thing happens: *"I
prophesied again."* Ezekiel held on; he resisted doubt.
Instead of being discouraged both at the skeletons and at the
corpses, he took it that God was with him. Alone with God—
he prevailed. *"He prophesied as commanded and the
breath came into them and they L-I-V-E-D!"*

But who today can say, *"I prophesied as I was commanded, and they L-i-v-e-d"?* We boys can get crowds. Our
slick advertising, artistry, and strutting—our radio, music,
build up, and what have you—see to that. Why brethren, we
don't even know whether or not He has commanded us to
enter the ministry. Have we a pain in our hearts for perishing
men? Does the toll of eighty-five people dying without Christ
every minute turn our moisture into drought, take away our
garment of praise, or give us the spirit of heaviness? Can we
at this moment look up into the face of the living God (for
He is looking down on us) and say, "Woe is unto me if I
preach not the Gospel"? Can we actually say, "The Spirit of
the Lord God is upon me" anointing me to preach? Do we
count in hell? I mean, Would demons ever say, "Jesus I know,
and Pastor _____ I know!" Or, as we preach, do they
say, "But who are ye?" – AS IF MEN HAVE SOME KIND OF POWER!

The political crystal-gazers give us no cheerful predic-
tions, and the world's senior statesmen are whistling to
keep up their courage. John Citizen stands bewildered as a

spectator, seeing the Russellites, the Millennial Dawnists, and Jehovah's Witnesses peddling their poison at his door. Christian Science—which is neither Christian nor yet scientific—jostles with the Roman Catholics and Seventh Day Adventists to claim their right to lead him to heaven. John Citizen has heard of the Gospel with the hearing of the ear, but his eyes have *never* seen and his soul has *never* felt the power of a divine visitation. He has every right to ask, "Where is their God?" What shall we answer him?

One of the most painful things I know is to face up to truth. We are well conditioned to doctrine. Most of us know what the average preacher will say next. But a razor is blunt, compared to Spirit-edged truth. Ministers, and others in different parts of the world, all seem to have the same note of mourning, because of the ineffectiveness to a lasting degree of modern evangelism (even though it be fundamental)— flash-bulb evangelism we might call it—brilliant for the moment, but ah! but . . . !

Maybe we have a breath of life—of revival—in the churches, but we are not getting awakenings amongst the godless millions. We do get special trainloads, mainly of believers or church-goers, to our mass evangelistic efforts, but we need a General Booth to get to the up-and-outs, as well as to the down-and-outs.

The old saints used to sing,

"Blest are the men of broken heart,
Who mourn for sin with inward smart."

Herein are three very vital issues: *Broken Hearts, Mourning,* and *Sin.* First, "a broken and a contrite heart God will not despise"; in fact, God only uses broken things. For example, Jesus took the lad's bread and brake it; then, and only then, could it feed the crowd. The alabaster box was broken; only then could its fragrance escape and fill the house—and the world. Jesus said, "This is My body which was broken for you." If such was the way the Master went, should not the servant tread it still? For in saving our lives, we not only lose *them*, but we lose other people's too.

And next, mourning for sin! Jeremiah cried, "Oh that my head were waters," while the Psalmist says, "Rivers run down my eyes continually." Dear brethren, our eyes are dry because our hearts are dry. We live in a day when we can have piety without pity. It is passing strange. When a couple of struggling Salvation Army officers wrote to William Booth telling him they tried every way to get a move and failed, he sent this terse reply, "Try tears!" They did. And they had revival. ⌐ GIMMICK!

Bible schools don't teach "tears." They really cannot, of course. This is Spirit-taught; and a preacher, however weighed down with degrees and doctorates, has not gotten far unless he knows soul-bitterness over the sin of this day. A repeated cry of David Livingstone was, "Lord, when will the wounds of this world's sin be healed?" But are we grief-stricken in prayer? Do *we* soak *our* pillows, as John Welch did, in *our* soul travail? The scholarly Andrew Bonar lay on his bed on a Saturday night in Scotland, and as people below tramped the streets from the taverns and shows, he used to call from his tortured heart: "Oh! they perish, they perish!" Alas, brethren, we have not so learned Christ. Many of us know only a slick, tearless, passionless, soulless round of preaching, which passes for the minister's office these days.

Thirdly, what of sin? "Fools mock at it," says the Book. (Only fools would do so.) The Schoolmen of the Church have classified "seven deadly sins." We know, of course, that they are wrong, for all sin is deadly. Those seven sins are the womb out of which seventy times seventy million sins have been born. They are "the seven heads" of *one* monster, which is devouring this generation at a terrifying rate. We face a pleasure-doped youth, who couldn't care less about God. Cocksure with a pseudo-intellectualism, and insulated with a cultivated indifference to spiritual things, they also, alas, flaunt the accepted standards of morality.

It would be comic, if it were not tragic, to read that a certain film star (who is closely associated with scanty dress) refused to see the premiere of her own picture because she was upset at some of the indecent strips in it. (There is a demand for this stuff, hence the supply.) Remember that in Greek mythology, Augeas was king of the Epeians and noted for his immense wealth of herds, including twelve white bulls, sacred to Helios. For many years the stable for these bulls remained uncleaned. Then Eurytheus imposed upon Heracles the task of cleaning out all his stalls in one day. This Heracles did by turning loose through them the rivers Alpheus and Peneus.

Even so, to our knees, O Christians! Desist the folly of sprinkling today's individual and international iniquity with theological rose water! Turn loose against this putrefaction those mighty rivers of weeping, of prayer, and of unctionized preaching until all be cleansed.

> There is sin in the camp. There is treason today!
> > Is it in me? Is it in me?
> There is cause in our ranks for defeat and delay;
> > Is it, O Lord, in me?
> Something of selfishness, garments or gold,
> Something of hindrance in young or in old,
> Something why God doth His blessing withhold;
> > Is it, O Lord, in me?
> > Is it in me? Is it in me?
> > Is it, O Lord, in me?

Power from on high is the supreme need of today.
—CHARLES G. FINNEY

If Christ waited to be anointed before He went to preach,
no young man ought to preach until he, too, has been
anointed by the Holy Ghost.
—F. B. MEYER

Beware of reasoning about God's Word—obey it.
—OSWALD CHAMBERS

I cannot work my soul to save,
For that my Lord hath done;
But I will work like any slave,
For love of God's dear Son.
—UNKNOWN

Tell me in the light of the Cross, isn't it a scandal
that you and I live today as we do?
—ALAN REDPATH

As soon as we cease to bleed, we cease to bless.
—DR. J. H. JOWETT

CHAPTER SIX

Revival Tarries—Because

Harnack defined Christianity as "a very simple but very sublime thing: To live in time and for eternity *under the eye of God* and by His help."

Oh that believers would become eternity-conscious! If we could live every moment of every day under the eye of God, if we did every act in the light of the judgment seat, if we sold every article in the light of the judgment seat, if we prayed every prayer in the light of the judgment seat, if we tithed all our possessions in the light of the judgment seat, if we preachers prepared every sermon with one eye on damned humanity and the other on the judgment seat—then we would have a Holy Ghost revival that would shake this earth and that, in no time at all, would liberate millions of precious souls.

The heady, high-minded, incontinent truce-breakers of this hour, the tottering of thrones, the smoldering fires of Communism, and the bid for world dominion that Rome makes should fill us with alarm. It has been well said that there are only three classes of people in the world today: those who are afraid, those who do not know enough to be afraid, and those who know their Bibles. Sodom, which had no Bible, no preachers, no tracts, no prayer meetings, no churches, perished. How then will America and England be spared from the wrath of the Almighty, think you? We have millions of Bibles, scores of thousands of churches, endless preachers—and yet what sin!

Men build our churches but do not enter them, print our Bibles but do not read them, talk about God but do not believe Him, speak of Christ but do not trust Him for salvation, sing our hymns and then forget them. How are we going to come out of all this?

Almost every Bible conference majors on today's Church being like the Ephesian Church. We are told that, despite our sin and carnality, we are seated with Him. Alas, what a lie! We are Ephesians all right; but, as the Ephesian Church in the Revelation, we have "left our first love!" We appease sin—but do not oppose it. To such a cold, carnal, critical, care-cowed Church, this lax, loose, lustful, licentious age will never capitulate. Let us stop looking for scapegoats. The fault in declining morality is not radio or television. The whole blame for the present international degeneration and corruption lies at the door of the Church! It is no longer a thorn in the side of the world. Yet, it has not been in times of popularity but of adversity that the true Church has always triumphed. It is passing strange that we are so "simple" as to believe that the Church is presenting to men the New Testament standard of Jesus by such a substandard of Christian living.

Why does revival tarry? The answer is simple enough—*because evangelism is so highly commercialized.* The tithes of widows and of the poor are spent in luxury-living by many evangelists. The great crowds, great lines of seekers, great appreciation by the mayor, etc., are shouted to high heaven. All get publicity—except the love-offering! The poor dupes who give "think they do God service," while all they are doing is keeping a big-reputationed, small-hearted preacher living in Hollywood style.

Preachers who have homes and cottages by the lake, a boat on that lake, and a big bank balance, still beg for more. With such extortioners and unjust men, can God entrust Holy Ghost revival? These dear, doll-like preacher-boys no longer change their suits once a day, but two or three times a day. They preach the Jesus of the stable, but themselves live in swank hotels. For their own lusts they bleed the audience financially in the name of the One who had to borrow a penny to illustrate His sermon. They wear expensive Hollywood suits in honor of One who wore a peasant's robe. They feast on three-dollar steaks in remembrance of the One who fasted alone in the desert. Today an evangelist is not only worthy of his hire (so he thinks), but of compound interest. How fearful will all this be in the judgment morning!

Revival tarries *because of cheapening the Gospel.* We now have church hymns played strictly to dance tempo on our sacred records and over the radio, as well as in the churches. We have the precious blood of Jesus set to "boogie woogie" time. Imagine! We have the Holy Ghost syncopated! The platform has become a shopwindow to display our gifts, and the "visiting team" look like a mannequin parade. I would as soon expect a frog to sit down and play Beethoven's Moonlight Sonata as expect to see some of the slick preachers of this hour preach with an anointing that would cause godly fear among the people. The evangelists today are very often prepared to be anything to anybody as long as they can get somebody to the altar for something. They glibly call out: "Who wants help? Who wants more power? Who wants a closer walk with God?" Such a sinning, repenting "easy believeism" dishonors the blood and prostitutes the altar. We must alter the altar, for the altar is a place to die on. Let those who will not pay this price leave it alone!

Revival tarries *because of carelessness*. At the altar, too little time is spent with those souls who come to do eternal business. The evangelist is happy seeing his friends; and while sinners groan at the altar, he is drinking in the rich cream of men's praises. Thus America and England are strewn with spiritual derelicts, confused and confounded.

Revival tarries *because of fear*. As evangelists, we are tight-lipped about the spurious religions of the day, as if there were more than one name whereby men must be saved. But Acts 4:12 is still in the Scriptures—"there is *none other name* under heaven." To the modern preacher, does this seem tinged with bigotry?

Elijah mocked the prophets of Baal and sneered with derisive scorn at their impotence. Better to run out in the dark (as Gideon did) and cut down groves to false gods— than fail to do the will of God. The Christless cults and deity-dishonoring mushroom religions of this midnight hour tempt the Lord God. Will no one sound the alarm? We are not Protestants any more—just "non-Catholics"! Of what and of whom do we protest? Were we half as hot as we think we are, and a tenth as powerful as we say we are, our Christians would be baptized in blood, as well as in water and in fire.

Wesley saw the doors of the English churches closed against him, and Rowland Hill says of him, "He and his lay-lubbers—his ragged legion of preaching tinkers, scavengers, draymen, and chimney sweepers, etc.—go forth to poison the minds of men." What scurrilous language! But Wesley feared neither men nor devils. If Whitefield was burlesqued on the English stage in the basest way, and if, in the New Testament, Christians were stoned and suffered every ignominy, how is it then, since sin and sinners have not changed, that we preachers no longer raise the wrath of hell? Why are we so icily regular, so splendidly null? We can have riots without revival. But in the light of the Bible and Church History, where can we have revival without riots?

Revival tarries *because we lack urgency in prayer.* A famed preacher entered a conference the other day with these words, "I have come to this conference with a great burden for prayer on my heart. Will those who will share this with me, please raise their hands; and let none of us be hypocrites." There was a good response. But later in the week when a half night of prayer was called, the big preacher went to bed. Not much of a hypocrite! Integrity has passed away! All is superficial! The biggest single factor contributing to delayed Holy Ghost revival is this omission of soul travail. We are substituting propaganda for propagation. How insane! The New Testament adds a valuable postscript concerning Elijah when James 5:17 says "he prayed!" Had it not been for that, we should have seized the Old Testament story and, noting the omission of prayer, have said: "Elijah prophesied."

We have not yet resisted unto blood in prayer; nay, we "do not even get a sweat on our souls," as Luther put it. We pray with a "take-it-or-leave-it" attitude; we pray chance prayers; we offer that which costs us nothing! We have not even "strong desire." We rather are fitful, moody, and spasmodic.

The only power that God yields to is that of prayer. We will write about prayer-power, but not fight while in prayer. A title, undeniably true of the Church today, would be *"We Wrestle Not!"* We will display our gifts, natural or spiritual; we will air our views, political or spiritual; we will preach a sermon or write a book to correct a brother in doctrine. But who will storm hell's stronghold? Who will say the devil nay?

Who will deny himself good food or good company or good rest that hell may gaze upon him wrestling, embarrassing demons, liberating captives, depopulating hell, and leaving, in answer to his travail, a stream of blood-washed souls?

Finally, revival tarries *because we steal the glory that belongs to God.* Listen to this and wonder: Jesus said, "I receive not honour from men" and "How can ye believe, which receive honour one of another, and seek not the honour that cometh from God only?" (John 5:41, 44). Away with all fleshly backslapping and platform flattery! Away with this exalting of *"My* radio program," *"My* church," *"My* books!" Oh, the sickening parade of flesh in our pulpits: "We are greatly privileged, etc." Speakers (who are there really *by grace alone)* accept all this, nay—even expect it! The fact is that when we have listened to most of these men, we would not have known they were great if they had not been announced so!

POOR GOD! He does not get much out of it all! Then why doesn't God fulfill His blessed and yet awful promise and spew us out of His mouth? We have failed. We are filthy. We love men's praise. We "seek our own." "O God, lift us out of this rut and this rot! Bless us with breakings! Judgment must begin with us preachers!"

The Gospel is not an old, old story, freshly told. It is a fire in the Spirit, fed by the flame of Immortal Love; and woe unto us, if, through our negligence to stir up the Gift of God which is within us, that fire burns low.

—Dr. R. Moffat Gautrey

The greatest miracle of that day (Pentecost) was the transformation wrought in those waiting disciples. Their fire-baptism transformed them.

—Samuel Chadwick

The sign of Christianity is not a cross but a tongue of fire.

—Samuel Chadwick

The Gospel is a fact; therefore tell it simply.
The Gospel is a joyful fact; therefore tell it cheerfully.
The Gospel is an entrusted fact; therefore tell it faithfully.
The Gospel is a fact of infinite moment;
therefore tell it earnestly.
The Gospel is a fact of infinite love;
therefore tell it feelingly.
The Gospel is a fact of difficult comprehension to many;
therefore tell it with illustration.
The Gospel is a fact about a Person;
therefore preach Christ.

—Archibald Brown

True preaching is the sweating of blood.

—Dr. Joseph Parker

CHAPTER SEVEN

Is Soul-Hot Preaching a Lost Art?

Centuries have passed since the Swiss Reformer Oecolampadius forged the phrase, "How much more would a few good and fervent men affect the ministry than a multitude of lukewarm ones!" The passing of time has not taken the sting from this statement. We need more "good and fervent preachers." Isaiah was one such, with his "woe" of confession—"Woe is me! for I am undone; because I am a man of unclean lips, and I dwell in the midst of a people of unclean lips." And Paul was another such, with his "woe" of commission—"Woe is unto me, if I preach not the gospel!" But neither of these ordained men had a larger concept of the magnitude of his task than had Richard Baxter of Kidderminster, England. Listen to him in answer to the taunts that he was idle: "The worst I wish you is that you had my ease instead of your labor. I have reason to take myself for the least of all saints, and yet I fear not to tell the accuser that I take the labor of most tradesmen in the town to be a pleasure to the body in comparison to mine, though I would not exchange it with the greatest prince.

"Their labor preserveth health, and mine consumeth it. They work in ease, and I in continual pain. They have hours and days of recreation; I have scarce time to eat and drink. Nobody molesteth them for their labor, but the more I do, the more hatred and trouble I draw upon me."

There is something of New Testament soul-culture about that attitude to preaching. This is the Baxter who ever sought to preach as "a dying man to dying men." A generation of preachers of his soul-caliber would rescue this generation of sinners from the greedy mouth of a yawning hell.

We may have an all-time high in church attendance with a corresponding all-time low in spirituality. It may have been that in the past liberalism was rightly cursed by many as the seducer of the people. Now T.V. is the scapegoat, getting the anathema of the preachers. Yet having said all this, and knowing that both indictments carry truth, may I ask us preachers a question: Have we to confess with one of old, "The fault, dear Brutus, is within ourselves"? To sharpen my scalpel and plunge it further into the quivering flesh of the pulpiteers: Has great preaching died? is soul-hot preaching a lost art? have we conceded to the impatient modern's snack-bar sermons (spiced with humor!) the task of edging men's jaded spiritual appetites? do we endeavor to bring "the powers of the world to come" into every meeting?

Consider Paul. With a powerful anointing of the Holy Spirit upon him, he went out to ransack Asia Minor, mauling its markets, stirring its synagogues, penetrating its palaces. Out he went, with the war cry of the Gospel in his heart and on his lips. Lenin is credited with coining the phrase, "Facts are stubborn things." See how right such a phrase is by looking at the achievements of this man Paul; then sicken at the compromise of our generation of Christians! Paul was not merely a citywide preacher but a citywide shaker, and yet he had time to knock on the doors along the street and to pray for lost souls in the street.

The playboys of yesterday are the payboys of evangelism. A top-line evangelist of my knowledge refused a contract of five hundred dollars a week for a four-weeks' preaching campaign. No wonder a modernist has declared that these men will weep for souls—if the price is right—aye, like Judas, they will be weeping when it is too late! May weakness in the pew be caused by wickedness in the pulpit?

I am increasingly convinced that tears are an integral part of revival preaching. Preacher brethren, this is the time to blush that we have no shame, the time to weep for our lack of tears, the time to bend low that we have lost the humble touch of servants, the time to groan that we have no burden, the time to be angry with ourselves that we have no anger over the devil's monopoly in this "end time" hour, the time to chastise ourselves that the world can so easily get along with us and not attempt to chastise us.

Pentecost meant *pain,* yet we have so much pleasure. Pentecost meant *burden,* yet we love ease. Pentecost meant *prison,* yet most of us would do anything rather than, for Christ's dear sake, get into prison. Perhaps Pentecost relived would get many of us into jail—Pentecost, I say, not Pentecostalism—and I am throwing no stones.

Imagine Pentecost in your church this Sunday: *You* are endued as was Peter, and under your word, brother Ananias is slain and his wife soon stiff beside him! Would the moderns stand for that? Again, here is a Paul, smiting Elymas with blindness. In these days *that* would bring a court case against any preacher. And even prostration, which has accompanied almost all revival preaching, would "get us a bad name." Is not that more than our tender hearts could take?

I am appealing again, as at the beginning of this article, for majestic preaching. The devil wants us to major on minors. Many of us in the "Deeper Life" bracket are *hunting mice*—while *lions* devour the land! What happened to Paul while in Arabia I have never been able to find out. No one knows. Did he get a glimpse of the new heaven and the new earth and see the exalted Lord reigning over all? I still do not know; but this much is sure, that he altered Asia, jaundiced the Jews, riled the Romans, taught the teachers, and pitied prison jailors. This man Paul, and another preacher called Silas, dynamited the prison walls—with prayer—and cost the taxpayers a load in order that they might get about the Master's business.

Paul the bond-slave, Paul the love-slave, having settled that he was the hardest soul God would ever have to deal with, strode out to shake regions for God. On his day he brought "the powers of the world to come," stayed Satan, and outsuffered, outloved, and outprayed us all. Brethren, to our knees again, to rediscover apostolic piety and apostolic power. Away with sickly sermonizing!

The Church has halted somewhere
between Calvary and Pentecost.
—J. I. BRICE

How shall I feel at the judgment, if multitudes of missed
opportunities pass before me in full review, and all my
excuses prove to be disguises of my cowardice and pride?
—DR. W. E. SANGSTER

O Living Stream! O Gracious Rain!
None wait for Thee, and wait in vain.
—GERHARD TERSTEEGEN

Revival—the inrush of the Spirit into the body
that threatens to become a corpse.
—D. M. PANTON

A revival of religion presupposes a declension.
—CHARLES G. FINNEY

CHAPTER EIGHT

Unbelieving Believers

One of these days some simple soul will pick up the Book of God, read it, *and believe it.* Then the rest of us will be embarrassed. We have adopted the convenient theory that the Bible is a Book to be explained, whereas first and foremost it is a Book to be believed (and after that to be obeyed).

The fact beats ceaselessly into my brain these days that there is a world of difference between knowing the Word of God and knowing the God of the Word. Is it not true that with the coming round of Bible conferences we hear only old things repeated, and most likely come away without any increase in faith? Perhaps God never had such a set of unbelieving believers as this present crop of Christians. How humiliating!

Are we mesmerized by spiritual wealth? Perhaps a penniless seaman might be tantalized and tormented to sail over the Atlantic, knowing that beneath him lies the *Lusitania* with ten million dollars in her holds—his for the taking! The only barrier is a mile or two of water! Even so, the Bible, the Christian's checkbook from the Lord of glory, says: *"ALL*

things are yours . . . and ye are Christ's; and Christ is God's."
I am finding a healthy dissatisfaction these days with the
poverty of us believers.

We rarely enter a prayer meeting without hearing the
familiar phrase, "Lord, thou *canst* do this," (stating some
particular need). But is *that* faith? No. That is but recogniz-
ing the attribute of God called omnipotence. I believe that
the living, unchanging Lord of glory *can* change into solid
gold this good-sized table at which I am typing. Changing
water into wine or wood into gold is all within the compass
of His power. But He changed water into wine *because of
need.* Right now I could use a million clean dollars (and not
a cent of it on myself) in a way that would not make me
tremble or blush in "that great day"; and so I believe that
there is genuine need. But, to say that He *can* do this does
not change the wood; it therefore leaves me unsupplied. Yet
when I move up and say, "He *will* change this table into
gold," my problem is solved.

We *all* know that "the greatest of these [faith, hope, and
love]" is *not* faith. But why overlook the lesser? Where is
there pure faith these days? What a travesty of interpretation of genuine faith there is right now! A familiar cry is: "We
believe that the Lord would have us broadcast over ten more
radio stations; we are looking to Him to supply our needs;
send us your letters before next week!" That may be faith
and hints, but it is not being shut up to God alone. We
Christians glibly quote, "My God shall supply *all* (tremen-
dous word!) your need"; but really, do we believe it?

Without lessening its value, an appendix could be added
to Hebrews Eleven and could include Hudson Taylor (foun-
der of the China Inland Mission), George Mueller, Rees How-
ells, and others who *"through faith"* did mighty works. In
this perilous hour I am weary of all our mighty *talk* about

our risen, wealthy LORD, and yet the trailing poverty of us sickly believers! God honors not wisdom nor personality but faith. *Faith* honors God. And God honors faith. God goes wherever faith puts Him. *Faith,* in a sense which I believe you will understand, localizes deity. *Faith* links our impotence to His omnipotence.

The scientific world has broken the *sound* barrier; the lax, lustful world around us screams out to us that men have broken the *sin* barrier; now, please God, may we move along and by simple, single-eyed faith, break the *doubt* barrier! Doubt delays and often destroys faith. Faith destroys doubt. The blessed Book does not say "if thou canst *explain* the Scriptures, all things are possible to him that explaineth." God being who He is will never be explained in time; nor, we think, will He try in eternity to explain either Himself or His ways. The Book which is as immutable as its Author says, "If thou canst *believe, ALL* (that unavoidable word again) things are possible to him that believeth."

We have often heard people say with a sense of injury (after they have been overlooked for a job they thought they were admirably suited for), "It is not *what* you know these days that matters, but *whom* you know." I do not pretend to know how real that reasoning is in the business world; but I am absolutely sure it is right in the spiritual realm. What we know *about* God these days is giving us a deep stream of shallow books and is filling our libraries. (We are not despising true learning, and certainly not that wisdom which comes from above.) But *what* we know is one thing; *whom* we know is quite another. Paul had nothing, but yet "possessed *all* things." Sublime paradox! Blessed poverty! This blessed man was loaded spiritually. Building Christ's empire and writing the oracles of the Lord never unbalanced him. Yet despite Paul's incomparable record, we find him toward the end of the journey still longing for more: "That I may know him, and the power of his resurrection, and the fellowship of his sufferings, being made conformable unto his death."

Much of the barrier to believers' translating the promises of God into fact before the eyes of men is that wretched thing called *self*. But Paul remembered when his old King Self was *dethroned and*—what is more—*crossed out* on a cross (Gal. 2:20). Then Christ was enthroned. And before we can be clean and ready for Him to control, self-seeking, self-glory, self-interest, self-pity, self-righteousness, self-importance, self-promotion, self-satisfaction—and whatsoever else there be of self—must die. *Who* a man is is not important; *What he knows* does not matter; but *what he is* to the inscrutable God is what matters. If we displease God, does it matter whom we please? If we please Him, does it matter whom we displease? What we can *be* in union with Christ is one thing; but what we *are* is quite another. I am terribly dissatisfied with what I am. If you "have arrived," then pity your weaker brother and pray for me.

There is a faith that is just natural, intellectual, and logical; there is a faith that is spiritual. What good is it to preach the Word, if, as we present it, there is no kindling faith to make it live? "The letter killeth." Shall we add death to death? The greatest benefactor of this generation will be the person who brings down on this strutting but stricken protestantism the inestimable power of the Lord. The promise still stands: "The people that do know their God shall be strong and do exploits." If any of us knows God, "then watch out, Lucifer!"

Until self-effacing men return again to spiritual leadership, we may expect a progressive deterioration in the quality of popular Christianity year after year till we reach the point where the grieved Holy Spirit withdraws— like the Shekinah from the temple.

—**Dr. A. W. Tozer**

No man is ever fully accepted until he has, first of all, been utterly rejected.

—**Author unknown**

No boasting for me . . . none!—except in the Cross of our Lord Jesus Christ, by which the world has been crucified to me and I crucified to the world.

—**Galatians 6:14 (Moffatt's Translation)**

If I had a thousand heads I would rather have them all cut off than to revoke.

—**Luther, at Diet of Worms**

I fear not the tyranny of man, neither yet what the devil can invent against me.

—**John Knox, in "A Godly Letter"**

The business of the truth is not to be deserted even to the sacrifice of our lives, for we live not for this age of ours, nor for the princes, but for the Lord.

—**Zwingli**

CHAPTER NINE

Wanted— Prophets for a Day of Doom!

Paul's head is already halfway into the lion's mouth. What of it? Before Agrippa this daring, dauntless disciple Paul has neither nerves nor reserves! He can be no "tongue-in-cheek" preacher anytime, or anywhere. Physical courage will make a man brave one way; and moral courage, which despises men's opinions whosoever they be, will make a man brave another way. Both these types of courage made Paul a *Christian Daniel* in a Roman "den of lions." Men may try to destroy a prophet's body, but they can *not* destroy the prophet.

The clock creeps up to midnight as I write, and a peep through the window reveals a sky of velvet blackness. Transfer this into the realm of politics and it is a sky without a guiding star. Put that midnight sky in the realm of morals and you must multiply it to gross darkness. Come now to the realm of religion; count your T.V. audiences for top-line evangelists; tell me how many "big tops" are operating in evangelism at the moment; quote me the "converts" of all last year's Gospel efforts; and when you are done, I shall shout, with the roar of a tornado, "The moon of revival has not yet risen on this hell-bound, Christ-rejecting, speeding-to-judgment generation." We don't "sit at ease" in Zion anymore. We have gone past that; we just sleep. In the church, pillars have given place to pillows.

As I began to say, Paul, as he stands before Agrippa, has his head half into the lion's mouth. With an awareness that the feet of pallbearers are not far away, he now "turns on the heat" until that wretched immoral King Agrippa stammers, "Thou almost persuadest me to be a Christian." Then Festus, a mere guest, forgets his manners and barges in with "Paul, thou art beside thyself; much learning doth make thee mad." Paul parries, "I am not mad, noble Festus." (I think the tone of his voice infers that the listening sinners *are* mad.)

But tell me, today when we preach the everlasting gospel, does anybody think that we are "raving" (as Rotherham translates *mad)* or going "insane" (as Weymouth translates it)? On the contrary, we have our love-offering in view, our big name to defend, our crowds to consider, and our extent of days to think over, don't we?

The Methodists in England have just finished their "Yearly Corporation of the People Called Methodists," a thing that John Wesley formed in 1784. It was held in Newcastle, England (1958). In spite of the colossal efforts of mass evangelism in the past two years and the boasted "lasting value of much follow-up work," it was acknowledged almost with tears that "the evangelistic candle" is almost guttered out. There are men among them large of mind, large of heart, and large of vision. Peep into the debating hall. Yes, there on his feet is Edwin Sangster—scholar, theologian, author, and now head of Methodism's Home Missions. He is not refuting the charge that Methodism is sick and (some add) nigh unto death. The man is moved and moving. Listen to him. I quote:

"We are combatting something deep in the soul of the nation. For this deep malady, we need some deep X-ray therapy that we have not found." He adds, "I think, with passion, that agnosticism is flourishing in Britain in place of the great religious revival for which Methodists so fervently hoped. Last year church members in Methodism fell lower than for 13 years, and no less than 100,000 children ceased to attend Sunday schools." (I chip in here, Could TV be a real factor in this declension?) "Every year for the last twelve years the number of ministers has declined; it fell by 276 in the past year." (Dr. Sangster wrote some twenty years ago, *Can Methodism be Reborn,* knowing even then there was some canker at the heart.) Let Edwin Sangster finish his tormenting lament: "We thought that, even if our numbers were smaller, we could count on the total conviction of the people who came. But even those in the pews are having their battle for faith."

And Methodists in England are not alone in their perplexed plight. Tell me, Australians, Is the position like that with you? And what of the Church in South Africa? Any declension? In America we have an all-time high in church attendance; but that goes for Jews, Catholics, Jehovah's Witnesses, too; and do not forget the jails are full to overflowing, and the divorce mills are jammed to standing room only.

Men—benign, but bad and bloody—rule in many of the high places of the earth. "Uneasy lies the head that wears the crown." The cry of the slaughtered dead must be "Dost Thou not judge and avenge our blood on them that dwell on the earth?" The cry of "the living" (I mean those *really alive* with God-indwelt life) must be, "Avenge me of mine adversary. And shall not God avenge his own elect, which cry to him day and night?" Surely the hour is approaching when grace is impossible, when vengeance is inevitable.

To whom much has been given much will be demanded. Millions walk in darkness because they have no light; but the democracies are great offenders in that they have had light, but snuffed it out with the "bushel of business" or the "bed of idleness." Surely this Sodom-like sin must merit Sodom-like judgment. "This was the iniquity of thy sister Sodom," says Ezekiel 16:49—"pride, fulness of bread, and abundance of idleness." We need prophets for this day of doom—holy men of God—to speak "as they are moved by the Holy Ghost." If He does not still move preachers, then we had better close down. But *He does* move them.

Neither Gideon nor anyone else gets into trouble because of his visions. It is actions that bring down the wrath of the offended powers. Let a Gideon slip out at midnight and cut down the groves of Baal; then hell releases its fury. Let John the Baptist call the priests *"vipers"* and rail at Herod's adultery, and he has signed his own death warrant. Certainly we need prophets for this day of doom, for look at the mounting interest in the false cults. *Newsweek,* Aug. 4th, 1958, says that Homer Knorr, president of the Watch Tower Bible and Tract Society, will take the Yankee Baseball Stadium this week, for 150,000 Witnesses will gather for a convention (their biggest ever—a sign of their growth). This eight-day conference will end with the baptism of 4,600 fanatical ministers, who are unpaid and would compass sea and land with their Christ-denying, man-concocted, Bible-twisting religion, to make another convert sevenfold more the child of hell. This makes you *think*—particularly after the above quotation of the all-time low in England of men for the ministry.

Can this organized but paralyzed system called Christianity cumber the earth much longer? Is Sangster right when he says we have not found an answer for the deep malady affecting the nation? (Would it not be more correct to say that we have scorned the old-time method of proclaiming repentance and regeneration and sanctification?) Tucked away in my heart is a stirring consolation; I share it with you. When God-given, heaven-sent revival does come, it will undo in weeks the damage that blasphemous Modernism has taken years to build. By the gale of the Spirit, the deceptive doctors of divinity will see swept away "the house which they built upon the sand" of human interpretations of the Bible. The head of humanity is sick and the heart faint. In the scheme of men, we are at the end of the line. Everything is "laid on" now for the superblast of the ages that will slice the earth in atomic destruction. Hell enlarges her mouth for the spoil which the filthy modernists have prepared as they have bartered the blood of Christ for "a mess of pottage" ("higher criticism"—so-called). With swollen heads and shrunken hearts, they will look at their folly.

Arm of the Lord, awake! put on strength! This is the hour for revival. This is the hour of doom. Where are the men of God? Prophets *may* have miracles, but they *must* have a message. In their own way, the bewildered worldlings are saying, Is there any word from the Lord? They know there is no intelligent word from any other source. Because God cannot lie, therefore Joel 2 and Malachi 3 will be fulfilled. "The Lord whom ye seek shall *suddenly* come to His temple." What comfort there! This moment drought; the next, deliverance. Ten minutes before John the Baptist arrived—no one knew that he was there. As it *was*, so I am sure it *will be*. God will get some man's ear and heart and will. Men, hidden in secret at this very moment, will utter soon, in the Spirit's might, the burning truths that this people must hear. Their words will burn as molten metal. With long patience, God awaits.

But when He arises, "Who may abide the day of his coming?" At the operation of the Spirit, men at this moment "drawing iniquity with a cart rope," will bend as corn before the wind. The Kremlin will tremble at the news of a supernatural operation in China. May God precipitate revival in China, Russia, Germany, etc.—lands scorched with the fire of militant Communism. For one reason, they need it so greatly; for another, our free nations need to be provoked, as Jonah was with Nineveh. Pharaoh finally wilted—under the assault of the ten plagues; and under Moses the prophet, the Israelites were led to victory. Today we have ten other new plagues—more sinister and effective and mighty than those (because worldwide and not confined just to Egypt); yet even these new plagues have not melted the heart of modern man but made it militantly wicked.

Have we no modern Moses? Can we suffer this generation to perish in the slave camp of moral bondage—and sit idly by, doing nothing about it? Are we to be mesmerized spectators, while Lucifer, with millions chained to his infernal chariot, sweeps many souls down the "broad way" to everlasting darkness? We need to rediscover the secret of those blessed men of whom the Word says, "They subdued kingdoms, [and] stopped the mouths of lions"—(that "lion" who goeth about today "seeking whom he may devour"). For this day of doom our pale, pathetic, paralyzed protestantism needs God-filled and God-guided men. Wanted—prophets of God!

A baptism of holiness, a demonstration of
godly living is the crying need of our day.
—**DUNCAN CAMPBELL**

To bring fire on earth He came;
Kindled in some hearts it is,
But O that ALL might catch the blaze,
And ALL partake the glorious bliss.
The baptism of the heaven-descended Dove,
My heart the altar, and Thy love the flame.
—**GEORGE CROLY**

Come as the fire, and purge our hearts
With sacrificial flame;
Let our whole soul an offering be
To our Redeemer's Name.
—**ANDREW REED**

The same church members who yell like Comanche
Indians at a ball game on Saturday sit like wooden Indians
in church on Sunday.
—**VANCE HAVNER**

There can be no revival when Mr. Amen and
Mr. Wet-Eyes are not found in the audience.
—**CHARLES G. FINNEY**

CHAPTER TEN

Fire Begets Fire

Men of prayer must be men of steel, for they will be assaulted by Satan even before they attempt to assault his kingdom.

Praying which is merely putting in a request sheet to the Ruler of the Universe is but the smallest side of this many-faced truth. Like everything else in the Christian's life, prayer can become lopsided. Prayer is no substitute for work; equally true is it that work is no substitute for prayer. In his masterly but little-known work, *The Weapon of Prayer*, E. M. Bounds says, "It is better to let the work go by default than to let the praying go by neglect." Again he says, "The most efficient agents in disseminating the knowledge of God, in prosecuting His work upon the earth, and in standing as a breakwater against the billows of evil, have been praying church leaders. God depends upon them, employs them, and blesses them."

Surely revival delays because prayer decays. Nothing do Satan or hell fear more than praying men. But to live well you don't have to live long. A man only twenty-eight years old may die a hundred years old in wisdom. The dragonfly rends his husk and harnesses himself in a clean plate of sapphire mail for a pilgrimage to the dewy fields *lasting but a few days;* yet no flowers on earth have a richer blue than the color of his cuirass. So in the spiritual sphere, the richest garments of the soul are spun on the looms of prayer and dyed in the travail that fills up the sufferings of Christ. Fellow missionaries envied Henry Martyn's spirituality. One says of him, "Oh to be able to emulate his excellences, his elevation of piety, his diligence, his superiority to the world, his love for souls, his anxiety to improve all occasions to do souls good, his insight into Christ and the heavenly temper!" These are the secrets of the wonderful impression he made in India. Martyn says of himself, "The ways of wisdom appear more sweet and reasonable than ever, and the world more insipid and vexatious." "The chief thing I mourn over," he adds, "is my want of power and lack of fervour in secret prayer, especially when I plead for the heathen. In proportion to my light, warmth does not increase within me." Does anybody feel like casting the first stone at Henry Martyn? Would we not all have to say that in intercession we lack "heat"?

By its very nature, fire begets fire. If other combustible material is about, fire will only spread its kind. "See how great a matter a little fire kindleth." *Fire* can never make *ice,* the *devil* certainly cannot make *saints;* neither can prayerless pastors produce warriors of intercession; yet one spark from an anvil may set a city on fire. From one candle, ten thousand others may take a light! From the matchless prayer life of David Brainerd, outstanding stars in the firmament of soul-winners have caught their initial light (like Carey, Payson, etc.).

William Carey read Brainerd's life story, and a dynamo started within the young soul-winner's breast, finally landing him on India's coral strand. At the flame of Brainerd's molten soul, the candle of Edward Payson's heart was lighted under God. Thus from just the diary of the pain-wracked, cowhide-clad apostle to the North American Indians, Payson caught the motivating inspiration, and began at twenty a prayer life that almost eclipsed Brainerd's. To add yet another soul-kinsman of Brainerd's, another master of prayer, who tottered into his grave at the "ripe old age" of twenty-nine years, we speak of Robert Murray McCheyne. This giant in prayer was first magnetized to this "greatest of all human offices that the soul of man can exercise" by reading about Brainerd.

Then another soul, the great Jonathan Edwards, watched Brainerd (while his daughter Jerusha wept), as the tides of consumption grew greater over Brainerd's body. Godly Edwards wrote: "I praise God that in His providence Brainerd should die in my house so that I might hear his prayers, so that I might witness his consecration, and be inspired by his example." When Brainerd was dying, Wesley was in about the prime of his spiritual conquest. Listen to Master Wesley talking to his conference in England. (Bear in mind here the other chapter where I quoted Dr. Sangster at this year's (1958) Methodist Conference in England.) Wesley said, "What can be done to revive the work of the Lord where it has decayed?" And then the relentless, tireless evangelist, who shook three kingdoms, answered his own question by saying, "Let every preacher read carefully the life of David Brainerd."

So there we have it. Let's line them up: Payson, McCheyne, Carey, Edwards, Wesley—men of renown, yet all kindled by one flame, and all debtors to the sickly but supplicating Brainerd.

The conflict of the ages is upon us. This unbiblical distorted thing called the church, that mixes with the world and dishonors its so-called Lord, has been found out for what it is, a fraud. The true Church is born from above. In it there are no sinners, and outside of it no saints. No man can put another's name on its member's roll; and no man can cross another's name off that roll. This Church—of which, bless the Lord, there is still a small remnant in the world—lives and moves and has its being in prayer. Prayer is its soul's sincere desire.

As the first atom bomb shook Hiroshima, so prayer alone can release that power which would shake the hearts of men. This cultured paganism at our doors, those idol temples, those fear-gripped, sin-mesmerized millions can only be moved *to* God as the Church is moved *of* God for their lost condition. With every possible guile that he knows, the devil would snatch us from the closet of prayer. For in prayer man is linked with God, and in that union Satan is baffled and beaten. Well he knows this; and so, if the closet is shut tightly, the mind is invaded with legitimate cares or with imaginations as big or more real than life. Here we need to plead our main defense—the blood. Another useful way to offset wandering thoughts and to help concentration is to pray audibly or to give some utterance at least, though it need not be loud.

Having thus moved and gained the mastery over Satan, our next power is in the "exceeding great and precious promises of God." Here we are on concrete foundation. Here are our trading currencies with heaven. Here God is pledged, and longs to hear us honor Him. Here we may be engaged in warfare not *with* God but *against* principalities, for Satan delights in loss no more than any other being. Souls of men are his treasures. Damned souls, doubting souls, drunk souls, disobedient souls, sick souls, religious souls, souls of the young, souls of the old, and all souls outside of the regenerating power of the Spirit are mastered by him, though the degrees of his mastery vary. Souls, in various degrees of spirituality, are special targets for his fiery arrows, but the "shield of faith" will brush them all off and, bless the Lord, leave us all unscathed. Prayer is not for defence. The shield of faith is for that. Prayer is our secret weapon. (It seems secret to many of the Lord's people. Who of us, despite all that we have read, claims to know much about this masterly work of prayer?) We do not conquer Satan by prayer; Christ conquered him two thousand years ago. Satan fools and feints, blows and bluffs, and we so often take his threats to heart and forget "the exceeding greatness of God's power to usward." The Master Prayer said, "I give you power over all the power of the enemy." That is the victory. The soul is drawn out in prayer. True prayer is a time-eater. In the elementary stages, the clock seems to drag; later, as the soul gets used to the holy exercise, time flies when we pray. Prayer makes the soul tender. Notice, we never pray for folks we gossip about, and we never gossip about the folk for whom we pray! For prayer is a great detergent. I am aware that the blood is the great soul-cleanser. But in prayer, if there is anything within of condemnation, the blood drawn from Emmanuel's veins will speak by the Spirit in mighty cleansing.

Satan would have us increase even in Bible knowledge, I believe, as long as we keep from prayer, which is the exercise of the instruction we have received through the Word. What use is deeper knowledge if we have shallower hearts? What use is greater standing with men if we have less standing with God? What use is personal physical hygiene if we have filthiness of the mind and of the spirit? What use is religious piety if we have soul carnality? Why strut with physical strength if we have spiritual weakness? Of what use is worldly wealth if we have spiritual poverty? Who can take comfort in social popularity if he is unknown in hell? Prayer takes care of all these spiritual maladjustments.

The soul that would be free from the false spiritual reckoning of this hour will need to steel itself to a closer walk with God, a calm and heavenly frame of mind. The aspirant for spiritual wealth and for the ear of God will know much loneliness and will eat much of "the bread of affliction." He may not know too much about family or social opposition; on the other hand, he may. But this is sure, he will know much of soul conflict, and of silences (which may create misunderstandings), and of withdrawal from even the best of company. For lovers love to be alone, and the high peaks of the soul are reached in solitude. The poet says,

> "I heard a call, 'Come follow,'
>   That was all.
> Earth's joys grew dim,
> My soul went after Him,
> I rose and followed—
>   That was all.
> *Will you not follow*
> *If you hear His call?"*

Could a mariner sit idle if he heard the drowning cry?
Could a doctor sit in comfort and just let his patients die?
Could a fireman sit idle, let men burn and give no hand?
Can you sit at ease in Zion with the world
around you DAMNED?

—LEONARD RAVENHILL

Give me the love that leads the way,
The faith that nothing can dismay,
The hope no disappointments tire,
The passion that will burn like fire,
Let me not sink to be a clod:
Make me Thy fuel, Flame of God.

—AMY WILSON CARMICHAEL

. . . among whom ye shine as lights in the world;
holding forth the word of life. . . .

—PHILIPPIANS 2:15-16

Ye are the light of the world. . . .

—MATTHEW 5:14

CHAPTER ELEVEN

Why Don't They Stir Themselves?

America cannot fall—because she is already fallen! This goes for Britain, too. She cannot go into slavery—because her people are fettered at the moment in the chains of self-forged, self-chosen moral anarchy. Here are millions, diseased morally, with no longing for healing. Here are men paying for shadows at the price of their immortal souls, men who not only reject the Substance, but who openly sneer at and caricature it.

An unprecedented tidal wave of commandment-breaking, God-defying, soul-destroying iniquity sweeps the ocean of human affairs. Never before have men in the masses sold their souls to the devil at such bargain prices. "There is none . . . that stirreth up himself to take hold of Thee" (Isa. 64:7). What hell-born mesmerism holds them? How does the spell bind? Who brainwashed them? Why don't they wake and stir themselves?

Directed by the devil, the world has given a new injection to the flesh. One of the signs of "the last days" is that "men are lovers of pleasures." (Note that it is in the plural.) And where is hell's broth stewed? In the breweries of the world. It is a lame argument that in some cases government subsidies are granted to help the breweries keep men employed. Breweries are maternity clinics that breed men-slayers operating with guns, and men driving on the highways while drunken. Courts deal with the *fruit* of liquor; revival would slay this deadly tree at the *roots*.

The mad merry-go-round of sensuality is filled with millions awaiting their turn for initiation into iniquity. When wrong is so sweet a morsel, the sin-soaked, sex-slain youth could not care less about doing right. One crowded hour of glorious "life"—so they argue—is worth a gamble on the speculation of the theologians' so-called "eternity."

Look for one bitter moment. Could anything be less intelligent and unmanly than a drinking match? The prize winner is the last man still standing on his feet when all others, grunting like hogs, have fallen to the floor, unconscious in drink. This is a sport not of stone-age men of the Baliem Valley, but of the new intellectuals, satiated in body, stained in soul, and recklessly abandoned to iniquity!

Loaded with lechery, gutted with gambling, damned in drink, such men (who are adult in body, but moral imbeciles) whine out Lord Byron's lament:

> "I now have ashes where once I had fire,
> The soul in my body is dead;
> The thing I once loved, I now merely admire,
> My heart is as gray as my head."

If the Church had something vital and victorious to offer, these men who choose golf clubs by day and night clubs by night might be drawn from these fleshpots.

Since in their freedom men will not heed God, will He have to enslave to Communism the mighty millions of America that they might have time to remember His *day,* His *way,* and His *Son?* Better to die bound in body and free in spirit than free in body and bound in soul!

We stand aghast when we see fine men magnetized by science, but mystified by the Christian religion. When these have forsaken faith, they feed on films and football. In the light of "a thousand years being as one day," it has taken science a matter of mere seconds to bring us from the chuck wagon to the station-wagon, and from the covered-wagon to the Sputnik.

But after admitting that science does hold and attract when it drills a hole two miles deep into the earth for oil, and if there is none, does the same thing in the sea (as off the shores of Mexico)—let us seriously consider that science has diabolic and deadly forms too—even lobotomization!

Lobotomization is the inhuman, devil-inspired surgery spawned by science. As you consider science in this guise, be imaginative and yet a realist! For years this horrible operation on the brain has been a weapon in the hands of dictators. Hitler used it on millions of his own flesh and blood. Stalin is said to have turned over ten million of his slaves into living Zombies with this simple operation, which takes only five minutes to perform. Afterwards the victim is said to be irrevocably insane.

The patient is strapped to an operating table, the straps tight and very strong. Electrodes are attached to the temples, three jolts of electricity are shot through the patient's brain, enough to start violent convulsions which finally give way to anesthetic coma. The doctor then takes his leucotomes (ice-pick-like instruments) and inserts them under the patient's eyelids. With a hammer he drives through the eye sockets into the fore part of the brain, severing the prefrontal lobes of the brain from the rest of it. The result?—A

Zombie (for want of a better word).

Fifteen Zombies can be made by science in ninety minutes. To add to this, we have the alarming news that there are probably 100,000 lobotomized people in the United States, according to George Conitz in Liberty League News. When enlightened men dehumanize other men in this fashion, it is time to stop and ask if the great Goddess of Science has not received too much veneration from men.

Keeping those lobotomized millions in mind, meditate on this from the pen of famed Bertrand Russell, whose "Principles of Logic" has made him the uncrowned king of modern philosophers: "Man now needs for his salvation only one thing: to open his heart to joy, and leave fear to gibber through the glimmering darkness of a forgotten past. He must lift up his eyes and say: 'No, I am not a miserable sinner; I am a being who, by a long and arduous road, has discovered how to ... master natural obstacles, how to live in freedom and joy, at peace with myself and, therefore, with all mankind.'"

Would it be hard to persuade yourself that this "false prophet" of peace is dedicated to deception, consciously or otherwise? The same Bertrand Russell has trouble in trying to accept the incarnation. But would the relatives of the massacred Hungarians think his message a gospel of hope?

This is an hour in need of burning hearts, bursting lips, and brimming eyes! If we were a tenth as spiritual as we think we are, our streets would be filled each Sunday with throngs of believers marching to Zion—with sacks on their bodies and ashes on the shaking heads, shaking at the calamity that has brought the Church to be the unlovely, unnerved, unproductive thing that she is!

If we wept as much in the prayer closet as devout Jews have done at the Wailing Wall in Jerusalem, we would now be enjoying a prevailing, purging revival! If we would return to apostolic practice—waiting upon the Lord for apostolic power—we could then go forth to apostolic possibilities! This is the hour when we are asked over and over again, "Is everybody happy?" God's purpose for us is not happiness, but holiness! Soberness has given way to silliness, even though Paul in writing to Titus warns both young and old, "Be sober."

We surely need again to climb Calvary's hill on our knees, to survey the wondrous Cross in an attitude of humiliation and adoration. The Church must first repent; then the world will break! The Church must first weep; then our altars will be filled with weeping penitents.

At the very pinnacle of his power, William James, a Professor of Medicine at Harvard University, was struck down by a mysterious malady. His nerves were upset. He had insomnia and deep depression, but knew no cure for himself. He dashed off to Europe. Would Berlin have the answer? No door of hope opened. What about Vienna? The same answer. Might not Paris shelter a cure? But the panacea was not there.

Despair was heightening. London was near, but his call was but an echo. Scotland had eminent sons in this field. But there was no balm in this Gilead either. Back to America he came, the thought of suicide dancing in his brain. At last a man of prayer and of great faith for healing was recommended. Faith healing was anathema to William James, the distinguished philosopher and famed psychologist. His acute mind and mental training strongly protested against going this way. But needs must. James went. The simple, unlettered man of God put his humble hands on William James' head, who later said, "I felt a mysterious energy thrilling and tingling through my body which was followed by a sense of peace; I knew I was healed!" To cure the raging ills of this maddened world, the "Abana of Science" and the "Pharpar of Politics" are more attractive to our stubborn wills and warped intellects than the wondrous Cross. But for mankind to be made whole, we shall have to be as humble as William James was by getting back to the Cross of Jesus and its life-giving stream.

I have need of nothing.
—The Laodicean Church

Their iniquity;—pride, fulness of bread,
and abundance of idleness.
—Ezekiel 16:49

Is the Spirit of the Lord straightened?
Are these His doings?
—Micah 2:7

The Church that is man-managed instead of God-governed
is doomed to failure. A ministry that is college-trained
but not Spirit-filled works no miracles.
—Samuel Chadwick

The man whose little sermon is "repent" sets himself
against his age, and will for the time being be battered
mercilessly by the age whose moral tone he challenges.
There is but one end for such a man—"off with his head!'
You had better not try to preach repentance until
you have pledged your head to heaven.
—Joseph Parker

CHAPTER TWELVE

The Prodigal Church in a Prodigal World

To take an over-all view of the Church today leaves one wondering how much longer a holy God can refrain from implementing His threat to spue this Laodicean thing out of His mouth. For if there is one thing preachers are agreed upon, it is that this is the Laodicean age in the Church.

Yet while over our heads hangs the Damoclean sword of rejection, we believers are lean, lazy, luxury-loving, loveless, and lacking. Though our merciful God will pardon our sins, purge our iniquity, and pity our ignorance, our lukewarm hearts are an abomination in His sight. We must be hot *or* cold, flaming *or* freezing, burning out *or* cast out. Lack of heat and lack of love God hates.

Christ is now "wounded in the house of His friends." The Holy Book of the living God suffers more from its exponents today than from its opponents!

We are loose in the use of scriptural phrases, lopsided in interpreting them, and lazy to the point of impotence in appropriating their measureless wealth. Mr. Preacher will wax eloquent in speech and fervent in spirit, serving the

Lord with vigor and perspiration to defend the Bible's inspiration. Yet that same dear man a few breaths later with deadly calmness will be heard rationalizing that same inspired Word by outdating its miracles and by firmly declaring: "This text is *not* for today." Thus the new believer's warm faith is doused with the ice water of the preacher's unbelief.

The Church alone can "limit the Holy One of Israel," and today she has consummate skill in doing it. If there are degrees in death, then the deadest I know of is to preach about the Holy Ghost without the anointing of the Holy Ghost.

In praying, we assume the unpardonable arrogance of crying for the blessed Spirit to come with His grace—but not with His gifts!

This is the day of a restricted and relegated Holy Ghost, even in fundamentalist circles. We need and say that we want Joel 2 to be fulfilled. We cry, "Pour out Thy Spirit upon all flesh!" yet add the unspoken caution, "but don't let *our* daughters prophesy, or *our* young men see visions!"

"Oh, my God! if in our cultivated unbelief and our theological twilight and our spiritual powerlessness we have grieved and are continuing to grieve Thy Holy Spirit, then in mercy spue us out of Thy mouth! If Thou canst not do something with us and through us, then please, God, do something without us! Bypass us and take up a people who now know Thee not! Save, sanctify, and endue them with the Holy Ghost for a ministry of the miraculous! Send them out 'fair as the moon, clear as the sun, and terrible as an army with banners' to revive a sick Church and shake a sin-soddened world!"

Ponder this: God has nothing more to give to this world. He gave His only begotten Son for sinners; He gave the Bible for all men; He gave the Holy Ghost to convict the world, and equip the Church. But what good is a checkbook if the checks be unsigned? What good is a meeting, even if it be fundamental, if the living Lord is absent?

We must rightly divide the Word of truth. The text *"Behold, I stand at the door and knock"* (Rev. 3:20), has nothing to do with sinners and a waiting Saviour. No! Here is the tragic picture of our Lord at the door of His own Laodicean Church trying to get in. Imagine it! Again, in the majority of prayer meetings, what text is more used than "Where two or three are gathered together in My Name, there am I in the midst"? But too often He is *not* in the midst; He is at the door! We sing His praise, but shun His person!

With a stack of books beside us and marginal notes in Bibles for props, we have almost immunized ourselves from the scorching truth of the changeless Word of God!

I do not marvel so much at the patience of the Lord with the stonyhearted sinners of the day. After all, would we not be patient with a man both blind and deaf? And such are the sinners. But I do marvel at the Lord's patience with the sleepy, sluggish, selfish Church! A prodigal Church in a prodigal world, is God's real problem.

Oh, we bankrupt, blind, boasting believers! We are *naked* and don't know it. We are *rich* (never had we more equipment), but we are *poor* (never had we less enduement)! We have need of nothing (and yet we lack almost everything the Apostolic Church had). Can He stand "in the midst" while we sport unashamedly in our spiritual nakedness?

Oh, we need the fire! Where is the power of the Holy Ghost that slays sinners and fills our altars? Today we seem much more interested in having churches air-conditioned than prayer-conditioned. "Our God is a consuming fire." God and fire are inseparable; so are men and fire. Every single one of us is now treading a path of fire—hell-fire for the sinner, judgment-fire for the believer! Because the Church has lost Holy Ghost fire, millions go to hell-fire.

The prophet Moses *was called by* fire. Elijah *called down* fire. Elisha *made* a fire. Micah *prophesied* fire. John the Baptist cried, "He shall *baptize* you with the Holy Ghost, and *with fire.*" Jesus said, "I am come to *send fire* on the earth." If we were as scared to miss *fire* baptism as we are to miss *water* baptism, we would have a flaming Church and another Pentecost. The "old nature" may dodge the *water* baptism, but it is destroyed in the *fire* baptism, for He shall "burn up the chaff with unquenchable fire." Until they were fire-purged, the miracle-working disciples who beheld His resurrection glory, were held back from ministering the Cross.

By what authority do men minister these days at home or overseas without an "upper room" experience? We have no lack of preachers of prophecy, but we are pitiably short of *prophetic* preachers. We make no plea for spiritual predictors and sensational prognosticators. There is now little scope left to foretell, for we have the Book and the unveiling of the Lord's mind in it. But we do need men to *forthtell.* No man can monopolize the Holy Ghost, but the Holy Ghost can monopolize men. Such are the prophets. They are never expected, never announced, never introduced—they just arrive. They are sent, and sealed, and sensational. John the Baptist "did no miracles"—that is, no rivers of derelict humanity swept down on him for his healing touch. But he raised a spiritually dead nation!

One marvels at our unblushing evangelists who announce that they have just had a wonderful revival with thousands thronging the altars, and then add, to soothe the staid fundamentalists, "but there was nothing sensational and no disorder." But can there be an earthquake without sensation? Or a tornado without disorder? Did Wesley's scorching ministry cause no upheaval? The Church in England slammed every door in the face of "a *man sent from God whose name was John*"—Wesley. But these "religious Canutes" did not keep back the tide of Holy Ghost revival.

This blessed man, Wesley, went away from Oxford University, having "failed completely," *conspicuously* is his own word (even with the brain of a scholar, the fire of a zealot, and the tongue of an orator), to lead others to the Lamb. Then came May the 24th, 1738, when John Wesley at an Aldersgate Street prayer meeting, was born of the Spirit; later he was filled with the Spirit. In thirteen years this fire-baptized man shook three kingdoms. And Savonarola shook Florence in central Italy until the face of "the mad monk" became a terror to the Florentines of his day, and a thing of derision to the religionists.

Brethren, in the light of the "bema seat," we had better live six months with a volcanic heart, denouncing sin in places high and low and turning the nation from the power of Satan unto God (as John the Baptist did) rather than die loaded with ecclesiastical honours and theological degrees and be the laughing stock of hell and of spiritual nonentities. Lampooning "liquor barons" and cursing corrupt politicians bring no fire down upon our heads. We can do both of these, and keep our heads and our pulpits. Prophets were martyred for denouncing false religion in no vague terms. And when we too see "lying religion" cheating men in life and robbing loved ones in death, or when we see priests leading them to hell under the banner of a crucifix, we should burn against them with holy indignation. Later, maybe, to lead the way to a Twentieth Century Reformation, we shall burn on martyr fires.

With tears, view this news: "Palsied Protestantism now hears the Roman Catholic priests commending Protestant evangelists!" In all conscience, could you picture the same religionists applauding a Luther, or sponsoring a Savonarola? "Oh! God, send us prophetic preaching that searches and scorches! Send us a race of martyr-preachers—men burdened, bent, bowed, and broken under the vision of impending judgment and the doom of the unending hell of the impenitent!

Preachers make pulpits famous; prophets make prisons famous. May the Lord send us prophets—terrible men, who cry aloud and spare not, who sprinkle nations with unctionized woes—men too hot to hold, too hard to be heard, too merciless to spare. We are tired of men in soft raiment and softer speech who use rivers of words with but a spoonful of unction. These know more about competition than consecration, about promotion than prayer. They substitute propaganda for progagation and care more for their church's happiness than for its holiness!

Oh in comparison with the New Testament Church we are so sub-apostolic, so substandard! Sound doctrine has put most believers sound asleep, for the letter is not enough. It must be kindled! It is the letter *plus the Spirit* which "giveth life." A sound sermon in faultless English and flawless interpretation can be as tasteless as a mouthful of sand. To rob Rome and cripple Communism we need a fire-baptized Church. A blazing bush drew Moses; a blazing Church will attract the world, so that from its midst they will hear the voice of the living God.

Let me burn out for God. After all, whatever God may
appoint, prayer is the great thing. Oh, that I
may be a man of prayer!

—**HENRY MARTYN**

Love is kindled in a flame, and ardency is its life. Flame is
the air which true Christian experience breathes. It feeds
on fire; it can withstand anything, rather than a feeble
flame; but when the surrounding atmosphere is frigid or
lukewarm, it dies, chilled and starved to its vitals.
True prayer MUST be aflame.

—**E. M. BOUNDS**

O for a passionate passion for souls,
O for a pity that yearns!
O for the love that loves unto death,
O for the fire that burns!
O for the pure prayer-power that prevails,
That pours itself out for the lost!
Victorious prayer in the Conqueror's Name,
O for a PENTECOST!

—**AMY WILSON CARMICHAEL**

CHAPTER THIRTEEN

Wanted—A Prophet to Preach to the Preachers!

To attempt to measure the sun with an inch tape could hardly be more difficult than attempting to measure John the Baptist by our modern standards of spirituality. At Jordan the anxious crowd asked concerning the newborn child, "What manner of child shall this be?" They were told, "He shall be *great* in the sight of the Lord."

Today we are prodigal with the use of this word "great," for we mistake *prominence* for *eminence*. In those days God was wanting not a priest nor a preacher, but men. There were plenty of men then, as now; but all were too small. God wanted a *great* man for a *great* task!

John the Baptist probably had not one qualification for the priesthood, but he had every quality to become a prophet. Immediately before his coming there had been four hundred years of darkness without one ray of prophetic light—four hundred years of silence without a "Thus saith the Lord"—four hundred years of progressive deterioration in spiritual things. With a river of beasts' blood for its atonement and with an overfed priesthood for its mediator, Israel,

God's favored nation, was lost in ceremony, sacrifice, and circumcision.

But what an army of priests could not do in four hundred years, one man "sent of God," *John the Baptist,* God-fashioned, God-filled, and God-fired, did in six months!

I share the view of E. M. Bounds that it takes God twenty years to make a preacher. John the Baptist's training was in God's University of Silence. God takes all His great men there. Though to Paul, the proud, law-keeping Pharisee of colossal intellect and boasted pedigree, Christ made a challenge on the Damascus road, it needed his three years in Arabia for emptying and unlearning before he could say, "God revealed Himself in me." God can fill in a moment what may take years to empty. Hallelujah!

Jesus said, "Go ye!" but He also said, "Tarry until!" Let any man shut himself up for a week with only bread and water, with no books except the Bible, with no visitor except the Holy Ghost, and I guarantee, my preacher brethren, that that man will either break up *or* break through and out. After that, like Paul, he will be known in hell!

John the Baptist was in God's School of Silence, the wilderness, until the day of his showing forth. Who was better fitted for the task of stirring a torpid nation from its sensual slumber than this sun-scorched, fire-baptized, desert-bred prophet—sent of God with a face like the judgment morning? In his eyes was the light of God, in his voice was the authority of God, and in his soul was the passion of God! Who, I ask, could be greater than John? Truly "he did no miracle," that is, he never raised a dead man; but he did far more—he raised a dead nation!

This leathern-girdled prophet with a time-limit ministry so burned and shone that those who heard his hot-tongued, heart-burning message, went home to sleepless nights until their blistered souls were broken in repentance. Yet John the Baptist was *strange in doctrine*—no sacrifice, ceremony. or circumcision; *strange in diet*—no winebibbing nor banqueting; *strange in dress*—no phylacteries nor Pharisaic garments.

Yes, but John was great! Great eagles fly alone; great lions hunt alone; great souls walk alone—alone with God. Such loneliness is hard to endure and impossible to enjoy unless God-accompanied. Truly John made the grade in greatness. He was great in three ways: *great in his fidelity* to the Father—training long years, preaching short months; *great in his submission* to the Spirit—he stepped and stopped as ordered; *great in his statements* of the Son—declaring Jesus, whom he had never seen before, as "the Lamb of God who taketh away the sin of the world."

John was a *"Voice."* Most preachers are only echoes, for if you listen hard, you will be able to tell what latest book they have read and how little of *the* Book they quote. To reach the masses we need a Voice—a heaven-sent prophet to preach to *preachers!* It takes broken men to break men. Brethren, we have equipment but not enduement; commotion but not creation; action but not unction; rattle but not revival. We are dogmatic but not dynamic!

Every epoch has been initiated by fire; every life, whether of preacher or prostitute, will end with fire—judgment fire for some, hell-fire for others! Wesley sang, "Save poor souls out of the fire and quench their brands in Jesus' blood." Brethren, we have only *one mission*—to save souls; *and yet they perish!* Oh! think of them! Millions, hundreds of millions, maybe over one thousand million eternal souls, need Christ. Without Eternal Life they perish! Oh! the shame of it! the horror of it! the tragedy of it! "Christ was not willing that *any* should perish." Preachers, people go by the millions to hell-fire today because we have *lost Holy Ghost fire!*

This generation of preachers is responsible for this generation of sinners. At the very doors of our churches are the masses—unwon because they are unreached, unreached because they are unloved. Thank God for all that is being done for missions overseas. Yet it is strangely true that we can get more "apparent" concern for people across the world than for our perishing neighbors across the street! With all our mass-evangelism, souls are won only in hundreds. Let an atom bomb come and they will fall by the thousands into hell.

To say that the sin of today has no parallel is without foundation. Jesus said, "As it was in the days of Noah, so shall it be also in the days of the Son of man." We find a graphic picture of Noah's time in Genesis 6:5, "God saw . . . the wickedness of man was great in the earth, and that every imagination . . . of his heart was only evil continually." So it was, evil without exception, *every* imagination; evil without mixture, *only* evil; evil without intermission, evil *continually.* As it was, so it is! Sin today is both glamorized and popularized, thrown into the ear by radio, thrown into the eye by television, and splashed on popular magazine covers. Churchgoers, sermon-sick and teaching-tired, leave the meeting as they entered it—visionless and passionless! Oh God, give this perishing generation ten thousand John the Baptists—to tear away the bandages put over our national and international sins by politicians and moralists!

Just as Moses could not mistake the sight of the burning bush, so a nation could not mistake the sight of a burning man! God meets fire with fire. The more fire in the pulpit, the less burning in hell-fire. John the Baptist was a new man with a new message. As a man accused of murder hears the dread cry of the judge, "Guilty!" and pales at it, so the crowd heard John's cry, *"Repent!"* until it rang down the corridors of their minds, stirred memory, bowed the conscience, and brought them terror-stricken to repentance and baptism! After Pentecost, the onslaught of Peter, fresh from his fiery baptism of the Spirit, shook the crowd until as one man they cried out: "Men and brethren, what shall we do?" Imagine someone telling these sin-stricken men, "Just sign a card! Attend church regularly! Pay your tithes!" No! A thousand times NO!

Unctionized by the Spirit's might, John cried, *"Repent!"* And they did! Repentance is not a few hot tears at the penitent form. It is not emotion or remorse or reformation. Repentance is a change of mind about God, about sin, and about hell!

Nature's two greatest forces are fire and wind, and these two were wedded on the Day of Pentecost. Thus, just like wind and fire, that blessed "upper room" company were irresistible, uncontrollable, unpredictable—Then their fire started missionary fires, quenched the violence of fire, lit martyr fires, and started revival fires!

Two hundred years ago, Charles Wesley sang

"O that in me the sacred fire
    Might now begin to glow,
Burn up the dross of base desire,
    And make the mountains flow!"

Dr. Hatch cried,

"Breathe on me, Breath of God,
    Till I am wholly Thine,
Until this earthly part of me
    Glows with Thy fire divine."

Holy Ghost fire both destroys, purifies, warms, attracts, and empowers.

Some Christians cannot say when they were saved. But I never knew a man yet who was baptized with the Holy Ghost and Fire and was unable to say when it happened. Such Spirit-filled men shake nations for God, like Wesley who was born of the Spirit, filled with the Spirit, and lived and walked in the Spirit.

An automobile will never move until it has ignition—fire; so some men are neither moved nor moving because they have everything except fire.

Beloved brethren, there is to be a special judgment for preachers; they shall receive the greater condemnation (James 3:1). Can it be possible that as they stand condemned before the bar of God, men will turn on some and say, "Preacher, if you had had Holy Ghost fire, I should not now be going to hell-fire." Like Wesley, I believe in the need for repentance in the believer. The promise of the Father is for *you*. Just now, on your knees in that lonely mission station, or by your chair in that comfortable home, or in the pastor's study crushed and almost ready to give up, make this your prayer:

> To make my weak heart strong and brave,
>   Send the fire.
> To live a dying world to save, send the fire.
> Oh, see me on Thy altar lay
> My life, my all, this very day;
> To crown the offering now, I pray:
>   Send the fire!
> —F. de L. Booth-Tucker

We have a cold church in a cold world *because the preachers are cold.* Therefore, "Lord, send the Fire!"

No hat will I have but that of a martyr,
reddened with my own blood.

**—Savonarola, when
rejecting a cardinal's hat**

Apostolic preaching is not marked by its beautiful diction,
or literary polish, or cleverness of expression, but
operates "in demonstration of the Spirit and of power."

—Arthur Wallis

There are three things I would have liked to have seen.
They are these:
1. Jesus in the flesh.
2. Imperial Rome in its splendor.
3. Paul preaching.

—Augustine

Most joyfully will I confirm with my blood that truth
which I have written and preached.

—John Huss at the stake

The primary qualification for a missionary is not love for
souls, as we so often hear, but love for Christ.

—Vance Havner

CHAPTER FOURTEEN

An Empire Builder for God

Had Saul met only a preacher and heard only a sermon on the Damascus road, he might never have been heard of again. *But he met Christ!* (Sermons and preachers can be avoided—they often are—but Christ can never be avoided.) Right there that day Saul's philosophy of life was met with Life Himself. This fire-eating religious zealot met the fire-baptizing Lord; and as a result, when Saul was changed, civilization took a turn for the better. (May it please Thee to do this again, Lord, today!) Though in his own sight, a rigid, lawkeeping, blameless Pharisee, Paul soon began to declare himself to be the chief of sinners in the sight of God. No wonder, for he was to the infant church what Herod was to the infant Christ—turning darkest hell into yet darker despair.

A man with an experience of God is never at the mercy of a man with an argument, for an experience of God that costs something is worth something, and does something. Paul's was not an experiment that day; it was an experience. Yet his encounter with the Holy One that day must have been as terrorizing as it was transforming. He had a blinding vision of the Lord "above the brightness of the [noonday] sun."

Thereafter Paul was blind to all earthly honor. "They shall not honor me who would not honor Thee," said F. W. H. Meyer. Saul's collision with Christ suddenly shattered his dream of intellectual kingship and beggared his earthly prospects. Thus stricken, he stepped down yet further to another ordeal with God—the stripping in the Arabian desert (of which things his lips are sealed).

And somewhere this empire-builder for Christ, with his colossal intellect and wonderful pedigree, accepted his Lord not only in substitution, but also in identification—"*I died* [in Him]." (To this truth we all render glib lip-service.) Paul also triumphantly affirms, "He *l-i-v-e-t-h* in me!" Grasp this truth with both hands. If we so testified, would friends shoot out the lip of mockery at us? This sold-out servant-of-the-Saviour arose from the ashes of his burned-up self to be the New Testament Samson, lifting off its hinges the gates of history, and turning Calvary's cleansing stream into the foul stables of Asian corruption. Blessed man!

Having found peace with God, Paul made war on all that was godless. He charmed the intelligentsia of Athens on his sweet lyre of the Gospel, ending his song abruptly by grasping the resurrection-trumpet, only to send the Athenians scattering—scarred and scorched by its truth.

But what made this man laugh at the frowning crags of Asia's barriers? Why did he die daily? What reason is there for his unmatched list of fortitude (II Cor. 11)? Wherein is the rational explanation that he should carry an oversized burden? The answer is not from any wild guess or imagination, but from the well-kept diary of his soul. Staggering as it is, he goes on record as saying, "[It is] not I, but Christ liveth in me" (Gal. 2:20). Ponder it! He does not declare that he believes in the virgin birth, or that he is sure the Lord rose again from the dead—though of course, he believed this—but "Christ is now living in me!" From the sickening depth of depravity ("no more I . . . but sin that dwelleth in me," Rom. 7:17), he is now asserting from the height of spirituality, "Not I, but Christ liveth in me" (Gal. 2:20). Precious exchanged life!

Paul's was an *exemplary life*. He was not a guidepost, but a guide. Listen to him, "Those things which ye have heard and seen in me, do" (Phil. 4:9). He was indeed a "living epistle."

Paul's was an *exceptional life*. Would anyone be stupid enough to claim that Paul's self-abnegation is ours? Is it not rather true of us, "All seek their own"? He was exceptional in that he wrote so many epistles, and founded so many churches. But read the list again in II Cor. 11. Is he trying to outsuffer the martyrs, or make a safe claim to be listed with the saints? Not a bit of it! Place, pedigree, and privilege are but dung that he may win Christ, and by his abiding obedience be found in Him. He was exceptional in suffering, which was often by the choice of others, but exceptional in prayer, too, which was by his own choice. If more were strong in prayer, more would be suited to suffer. Prayer develops bone as well as groan, sinew as well as saintliness, fortitude as well as fire.

Paul calls the Holy Ghost as a witness that he could wish himself *"accursed"* for his brethren (Rom 9:3). Madam Guyon prayed almost an identical prayer. Brainerd and John Knox were "men of like passions." When, brother, (or where), did we ever hear such a prayer offered in a prayer meeting? We cannot have big results from our small praying. The law of prayer is the law of harvest: sow sparingly in prayer, reap sparingly; sow bountifully in prayer, reap bountifully. The trouble is we are trying to get from our efforts what we never put into them.

Paul's was an *expanding life*. Many of us, alas, are happy to get the scraps that are left over from another man's ministry. But Paul built upon no man's foundation (I Cor. 3:10), for his brain was not so steeped in dogma that it became an ecclesiastical machine, merely grinding out the mysteries of metaphysics. He spent no wearying hours speculating upon Daniel's image. Neither did he hide away in some spiritual laboratory dissecting truth or labelling theological capsuls, nor yet complimenting himself on his ability to polish words for future creeds. The reason for this is as clear as the noonday.

Paul wrote no "Life of Christ"; He demonstrated it by his *"I am a debtor"* (Rom. 1:14). If humanly possible at all, his soul's honor was pledged to erase that debt. The cost might be prison, for it were better that he should be "the prisoner of the Lord" *for a few years* than that his fellow men should be the devil's prisoners in hell *forever*. Paul was committed to a complete and costly consecration: "Henceforth let no man trouble me" (Gal. 6:17). Paul was sold out to God. Every beat of his heart, every thought of his mind, every step of his feet, and every longing of his soul—all were for Christ and the salvation of men. He upset synagogues, had revivals and riots—either one or the other, sometimes both. (We seem to have neither.)

Though his revival party let him down—"all men forsook me" (II Tim. 4:16), he dropped into the "everlasting arms" and went on. He escaped assassination; but with his daily bread he had daily death, for he said, *"I die daily"* (I Cor. 15:31). Magnificent misery his!

The fruits of the Spirit were upon Paul; the gifts of the Spirit operated through him. He held citywide revivals while he patched tents to pay expenses! My brother preachers, aren't we a chicken-hearted group by the side of Paul?

Sometimes he almost starved! Yet when the table was full, he fasted. He wished everyone blessing, yet could wish himself accursed. With his revolutionary living and riotous theology, this "spectacle before men," this Christian filled with the Holy Ghost, is the redemptive counterpart of the fanatical devotee of the political religion of atheistic Communism. "People consumed by the inner fire of the Spirit are the counterpart in human life of the smashed atom which releases cosmic forces."

Paul, transformed, transported, and soon to be transplanted, reveals that we all could be "like him." Hear him as he stands before Agrippa—"I would to God, that not only thou, but also all that hear me this day were both almost, and altogether as I am, except these bonds." He does not say that he wishes all would write as he has done. Nor does he say that all would found churches by his example. Paul does not say "as I *did,*" but, "as I myself *am*" (I Cor. 7:7). The Spirit that filled Paul can so fill us that we, like him, can be identified with Christ in sacrifice if not in service.

Where will this end with you, my brother? I do not know. (Neither do angels or men.) But where it all *begins* is in an Exchanged Life whereby we no longer live—but *Christ Lives in us.* Paul lived gloriously and died triumphantly because in sacrifice and suffering he identified himself with Christ. So can we live and die, if we but will.

The only saving faith is that which casts
itself on God for life or death.
—**MARTIN LUTHER**

. . . That is why, at every point in history where the
Church of Christ has been carried on some wave of revival
back to reality and self-consecration, thousands of men
and women have rediscovered Paul, and have thrilled
again
to the music of his message.
—**DR. J. S. STEWART**

Tearless hearts can never be the heralds of the Passion.
—**DR. J. H. JOWETT**

Oh! for a heart that is burdened!
Infused with a passion to pray;
Oh! for a stirring within me;
Oh! for His power every day.
Oh! for a heart like my Saviour,
Who, being in an agony, prayed.
Such caring for OTHERS, Lord, give me;
On my heart let burdens be laid.
My Father, I long for this passion,
To pour myself out for the lost—
To lay down my life to save others—
"To pray," whatever the cost.
Lord, teach me, Oh teach me this secret,
I'm hungry this lesson to learn,
This passionate passion for others,
For this, blessed Jesus, I yearn.
Father, this lesson I long for from Thee—
Oh, let Thy Spirit reveal this to me.
—**MARY WARBURTON BOOTH**

CHAPTER FIFTEEN

Branded—For Christ!

In a certain sense all men are strangers to one another. Even friends do not really know each other. For to know a man, one must know all the influences of heredity and environment, as well as his countless moral choices that have fashioned him into what he is. Yet, though we do not really know one another, tracing the course of a man's life sometimes offers rich reward, particularly when we see the great driving forces which have motivated him. For instance, how greatly your life and mine would be benefited if we could experience the same surge of Christ-life that moved Saul of Tarsus, later called Paul, and plumb even a little the hidden depths of the meaning in his words, "I bear in my body the marks of the Lord, Jesus" (Gal. 6:17)!

One thing is sure about these words—they were an acknowledgment of Christ's ownership. Paul belonged to the Lord Jesus Christ—body, soul, and spirit. He was *branded for Christ.* When Paul claimed to bear in his body the five wounds of the Lord, he was claiming no "stigmata," as did Saint Francis of Assisi in 1224 A.D. It is not a bodily identification by outward imitation that Paul was speaking of, but a spiritual identification by inward crucifixion. He had been "crucified with Christ" (Gal. 2:20).

The marks of Paul's inward crucifixion were plainly evident. First of all, Paul was *branded by devotion to a task.* If, as tradition says, Paul was only four feet six inches in height, then he was the greatest dwarf that ever lived. He out-paced, out-prayed, and out-passioned all his contemporaries. On his escutcheon was blazed: "One thing I do." He was blind to all that other men gloried in.

Likewise, Calvin suffered vituperation because he sat all day over his *Institutes*—with never a flourish of his mighty pen to tell us of the glories of the Alps. And Pascal was bitterly criticized because apart from the immortal soul of man, he could see no scenery anywhere worth looking at. And by the same token, the Apostle Paul might be castigated for saying not a word about Grecian art or the splendor of the Pantheon. His was a separation to spirituality.

After the Athenian clash on Mars Hill, he poured contempt on the wisdom of this world, dying daily to the temptation to outwit and out-think the wise. His task was not that of getting over a viewpoint, but of overcoming the legions of hell!

Somewhere, most likely in Arabia, Paul's personality had been transfigured. Never, after that, was he listed as a backslider. He was too occupied with going on. It would have vexed his righteous soul to hear a congregation sing, "Prone to wander, Lord, I feel it!" Unsponsored, unwelcomed, unloved—made little difference to Paul. On he went—blind to every jewel of earthly honor, deaf to every voice of siren-ease, and insensitive to the mesmerism of worldly success.

Paul was also *branded by humility.* Moths could not corrupt this God-given robe. He never fished for praise with humility's bait, but in the long line of sinners put himself first (where we would have put him last). The old Welsh divine said that if you know Hebrew, Greek, and Latin, do not put them where Pilate did at the head of Christ—but put them at His feet. "What things were gain to me," says Paul, "these things I count as loss for Christ."

What a heart's-ease is the virtue of humility—the great joy of having nothing to lose! Having no opinion of himself, Paul feared no fall. He might have swaggered in the richly embroidered robes of the chancellor of a Hebrew school. But in the adornment of a meek and quiet spirit he shines with more luster.

Next, Paul was *branded by suffering.* Consider the things he mentions in Romans eight: famine, peril, nakedness, and sword (these belonging to acute discomfort in the body), and tribulation (perhaps of the mind), distress, persecution (of the spirit). Of all these sufferings the "little" minister partook.

This wandering Jew "made war" on all that made war on God and on the children of men. This prince of preachers and his foe, the prince of hell, spared each other no beatings. It was a free-for-all and no holds barred!

Look closely at Paul! that cadaverous countenance, that scarred body, that stooped figure of a man chastened by hunger, kept down by fasting, and ploughed with the lictor's lash; that little body, brutally stoned at Lystra and starved in many another place; that skin, pickled for thirty-six hours in the Mediterranean Sea! *Add* to this list danger upon danger; *multiply* it with loneliness, count in the one hundred and ninety-five stripes, three shipwrecks, three beatings with rods, a stoning, a prison record, and "deaths" so many that the count is lost. And yet if one could add it all up, it must be written off as nothing, because Paul himself thus consigned it. Listen to him: "Our light affliction, which is but for a moment. . . ." That's contempt of suffering, if you like!

Furthermore. Paul was *branded by passion.* A man must be in the dead center of God's will and walking the tightrope of obedience to call upon the Holy Ghost to bear witness to his witness. Yet Paul does this in Romans, chapter nine, verse one.

Oh, that from this wondrous flame every living preacher might capture just a little light! Beatings could not cast the flame out of him; fastings and hunger could not kill it; nor misunderstanding and misrepresentation quench its fire; waters could not drown it, prisons break it; perils could not arrest its growth. On and on it burned, until life ebbed from his body.

The living Christ who was within Paul (Gal. 2:20), as manifested by his soul-passion, was at once the despair of hell, the capital for enlarging the Church, and cheer to the heart of the Saviour (who was seeing the travail of His soul and was being satisfied).

Paul was *branded by love.* When Paul experienced becoming a "man in Christ," he developed the capacity for love. (Only maturity knows love.) How Paul loved! First and supremely, Paul loved his Lord. Then he loved men, his enemies, hardship, and even soul-pain. And he must have loved this latter particularly, else he would have shirked prayer. Paul's love carried him to the lost, the last, and the least. What scope of love! Mars Hill with its intellectuals, the synagogues with their religious traditionals, the market places with their prodigals—all these he yearned over and sought for his Lord. Love like a mighty dynamo pushed him on to attempt great things for God. Not many have prayed as this man prayed. Maybe McCheyne, John Fletcher, and mighty Brainerd, and a few others have known something of the soul-and-body mastering work of intercession motivated by love.

I remember standing by the Marechale once as we sang her great hymn:

> There is a love constraining me
>> To go and seek the lost;
> I yield, O Lord, my all to Thee
>> To save at any cost!

That was not just a lovely sentiment. It cost her prison, privation, pain, and poverty.

Charles Wesley seemed to be reaching on tiptoes when he said, "Nothing on earth do I desire, but Thy pure love within my breast!" More recently Amy Carmichael uttered the heartfelt prayer, "Give me a love that leads the way, a faith which nothing can dismay!" These men and women were certainly on the trail of the apostolic secret of soul-winning.

Great soul-winners have always been great lovers of men's souls. All lesser loves were only conquered by the greater Love. Great love to the Lover of their souls drove them to tears, to travail, and to triumph. In this evil hour, dare we love less?

> Let me love Thee, love is mighty
> Swaying realms of deed and thought;
> By it I can walk uprightly,
> I can serve Thee as I ought.
> Love will soften every trial,
> Love will lighten every care;
> Love unquestioning will follow,
> Love will triumph, love will dare!

Without any of their choosing, millions will be branded

for the Antichrist one day. Shall we shrink to bear in our bodies, our souls, and our spirits our Owner's marks—the marks of Jesus? Branding means pain. Do we want that? Branding means carrying the "slur" of the servant. Will we choose to be branded—for Christ?

I have begotten you through the gospel.

—**Paul**

O brother, pray; in spite of Satan, pray; spend hours in
prayer; rather neglect friends than not pray; rather fast,
and lose breakfast, dinner, tea, and supper—and sleep
too—than not pray. And we must not talk about prayer,
we must pray in right earnest. The Lord is near. He comes
softly while the virgins slumber.

—**Andrew A. Bonar**

It was seven years
. . . before Carey baptized his first convert in India.
. . . before Judson won his first disciple in Burmah.
. . . that Morrison toiled before the first Chinaman
was brought to Christ.
. . . declares Moffat. that he waited to see the first evident
moving of the Holy Spirit upon his Bechuanas of Africa.
. . . before Henry Richards wrought the first convert,
gained at Banza Manteka.

—**A. J. Gordon**

Prayer—the soul's blood.

—**George Herbert**

CHAPTER SIXTEEN

"Give Me Children or I Die"

Revival is imperative, for the sluice gates of hell have opened on this degenerate generation. We need (and we say that we want) revival. Yet, though slick, shallow saints of this hour would have heaven opened and revival delivered on the slot-machine method, God has not mechanized His glorious power to fit our time-geared religious machinery.

"We wish revival would come to us as it came in the Hebrides," said a pastor recently. But fellow servant, revival did not come to the Hebrides by wishing! The heavens were opened and the mighty power of the Lord shook those islands because "frail children of dust . . . sanctified a fast and called a solemn assembly," and waited tear-stained, tired, and travailing before the throne of the living God. That visitation came because He who sought for a virgin in which to conceive His beloved Son found a people of virgin purity in those souls of burning vision and burdened passion. They had no double motive in their praying. No petitions were colored with desire to save the face of a failing denomination. Their eye was single to God's glory. They were not jealous of another group who was outgrowing them, but jealous for the

Lord of Hosts, whose glory was in the dust, the "wall of whose house was broken down, and whose gates were burned with fire."

To draw the brooding Holy Ghost, a church group fundamentally sound in the Bible is not in itself a decoy. Beloved, we have thousands of such groups over the world. A girl of seventeen years and a boy of the same age may be equipped physically to parent a child, and even legally married. But does *that* in itself justify their offspring coming? Would they have financial security to cover all the need? And would they be mentally mature enough to train a child in the way he should go? Revival would die in a week in some "Bible" churches, for where are the "mothers in Israel" to care for them? How many of our believers could lead a soul out of darkness into light? It would be as sensible to have spiritual births in the present condition of some of these churches as to put a newborn babe into a deep freeze!

The birth of a natural child is predated by months of burden and days of travail; so is the birth of a spiritual child. Jesus prayed for His Church but then to bring it to spiritual birth He *gave* Himself in death. Paul prayed "night and day . . . exceedingly" for the Church; moreover, he *travailed* for the sinners. It was when Zion travailed that she brought forth. Though preachers each week cry, "Ye must be born again," how many could say with Paul "Though ye have ten thousand instructors in Christ, yet have ye not many fathers: for in Christ Jesus *I have begotten* you through the gospel"? So he fathered them in the faith. He does not say that he merely prayed for them; he implies that he *travailed* for them. In the past century if the physical birth rate had been as low as the spiritual birth rate, the human race would now be almost extinct. "We must pray to live the Christian life," we say; whereas the truth is that we must live the Christian life to pray. "If ye abide . . . ye shall ask" (i.e., pray). I know that "asking" includes making our requests for the salvation of loved ones, but prayer is more than asking. Prayer, surely. is getting us into subjection to the Holy Ghost so that He can work *in and through us.* In the first chapter of Genesis every thing that had life brought forth its kind. Then in regeneration should not every really born-again soul bring others to birth?

We evangelists get a lot of credit—and very often take what is not ours at all. A woman in Ireland who prays for hours, prays each day for this poor stammerer. Others tell me "Never a day passes but what I lay hold of God for you." They have brought to birth many that are credited to me, whereas I very often only act as the midwife. In the judgment we shall be amazed to see big rewards go to unknown disciples. Sometimes I think we preachers who catch the eyes of the public will be among those rewarded the least. For instance, I know men who today preach sermons which they preached twenty years ago—which no longer gender life. Such preachers used to pray; one of these admitted to me some time ago, "No, brother, I do not pray as much as I used to, but the dear Lord understands." Aye, He understands all right, but He does not excuse us because we are busier than He wants us to be.

It is true that science has alleviated some of the suffering that our mothers knew in childbirth; but science will never shrink the long slow months of child-formation. In the same way we preachers have also found easier methods of getting folk to our altars for salvation or for the filling with the Holy Ghost. For salvation, folk are permitted just to slip up their hand and, presto! the groaning at the altar is eliminated. For the filling with the Holy Ghost, men are told to "Just stand where you are while the evangelist prays for you, and you will be filled." Oh, the shame of it! Brother, before the miracle takes place, *true* revival and soul-birth still demand travail.

As the coming babe dislocates the body of the mother, so does the growing "body" of revival and soul-travail dislocate the Church. The mother-to-be wearies more as the time of the birth draws near (often spending sleepless but not tearless nights); so the lamps of the sanctuary burn the midnight oil as distressed, sin-carrying intercessors pour out their souls for a nation's iniquities. The expectant mother often loses desire for food and, in the interests of the one she will bear, denies herself certain things; so denial of food and a consuming love to lie quiet before the Lord seizes believers shamed by the barrenness of the Church. As women in pregnancy hide from public gaze (or used to do so) as the time of deliverance draws near, so those in travail of soul shun publicity and seek the face of a holy God.

It is very obvious that Jacob loved Rachel far more than he loved Leah, but yet the "woman's delight" was with Leah, for she had children. Consider how Jacob served fourteen years for Rachel, and yet that splendid devotion was no comfort to the woman stricken with barrenness. Undoubtedly Jacob proved his love by loading her with jewels, as the custom of the day was; but external nonentities were comfortless. And though Rachel was beautiful to look upon, for her son-less state she found no compensation in her own beauty or the admiration of others. The terrible truth remained that Leah had four laughing lads about her skirts; but at unfruitful Rachel men mocked and women shot out the lip. I can imagine Rachel—with eyes more red from weeping than ever Leah's were, and with hair dishevelled and voice hoarse with groaning—coming before Jacob, annoyed about her sterility, humiliated to despair by her condition, and crying with a piercing cry, "Give me children or else I die!" (Gen. 30:1). That cry tore his heart as a sword would tear his flesh.

To spiritualize this, her praying was not routine but desperate, for she was gripped with grief, stunned with shame, and bowed low in barrenness. Preacher, if your soul is barren, if tears are absent from your eyes, if converts are absent from your altar, then take no comfort in your popularity; refuse the consolation of your degrees or of the books you have written! Sincerely but passionately invite the Holy Ghost to plague your heart with grief because you are spiritually unable to bring to birth. Oh, the reproach of our barren altars! Has the Holy Ghost delight in our electric organs, carpeted aisles, and new decorations if the crib is empty? Never! Oh that the deathlike stillness of the sanctuary could be shattered by the blessed cry of newborn babes!

There is no pattern for revival. Though babes are everywhere born by the same process, how different the babes themselves are—all new! no repeats! By the very same process of soul-grief and protracted prayer and burden because of barrenness, revivals of all ages have come—yet how different the revivals themselves have been!

Jonathan Edwards lacked no congregations and had no financial worries. But spiritual stagnation haunted him. The blemish of birth bankruptcy so buckled his knees and smote his spirit that his grief-stricken soul clung to the mercy seat in sobbing silence until the Holy Ghost came upon him. The Church and the world know the answer to his victorious vigil. The vows he made, the tears he shed, the groans he uttered are all written in the chronicles of the things of God. Edwards, Zinzendorf, Wesley, etc., were spiritual kinsmen (for there is an aristocracy of the Spirit, as well as of the flesh). Such men despised hereditary honors and sought the accolade of the Holy Ghost.

Political and military histories are wrapped up around individual men. History is sprinkled with the names of men who invested themselves with certain power and often made the world to tremble. Think of that evil genius Hitler. What kings he overthrew! what governments he tottered! what millions of graves he filled! To our age he was a bigger scourge than ten plagues. Hitler had one thing to do, and—he did it! The Bible says that in the last days when wicked men do wickedly, "the people that do *know their God* shall be strong and do exploits." Not those who sing about God, not those who write or preach about God, but they that *know their God* shall be strong and do exploits. Not talking about food will fill the stomach; not speaking of knowledge will make us wise; not talking of God means that the energies of the Holy Ghost are within us. We do well to ponder the fact that revival comes as a result of a cleansed section of the Church, bent and bowed in supplication and intercession. It views an age shackled with false religion and sickened at the sight of perishing millions; then they wait—perhaps days, weeks, and even months until the Spirit moves upon them, and heaven opens in revival blessing.

Women of the Bible who had been barren brought forth its noblest children: *Sarah,* barren until ninety years of age, begat Isaac; *Rachel's* cutting cry, "Give me children or I die!" was answered, and she bore Joseph, who delivered the nation. *Manoah's wife* bare Samson, another deliverer of the nation. *Hannah,* a smitten soul, after sobbing in the sanctuary and vowing vows and continuing in prayer, ignored Eli's scorn, poured out her soul, and received her answer in Samuel, who became the prophet of Israel. The barren and widowed *Ruth* found mercy and bare Obed, who begat Jesse, the father of David, of whose line came our Saviour. Of *Elizabeth,* stricken in years, came John the Baptist, of whom

Jesus said there was no greater prophet born of women. If shame of childlessness had not subdued these women, what mighty men would have been lost!

As a child conceived suddenly leaps to life, so with revival. In the sixteenth century Knox parodied Rachel's prayer, crying, "Give me Scotland or I die!" Knox died, but while Scotland lives, Knox will live. Zinzendorf, chagrined and shamed at the loveless, fruitless state of the Moravians, was melted and motivated by the Holy Ghost until—*suddenly* revival came at about eleven o'clock on the Wednesday morning of August 13, 1727. Then began the Moravian revival, in which a prayer meeting was born that we are told lasted one hundred years. From that meeting came a missionary movement that reached the ends of the earth.

The Church of our day should be pregnant with passionate propagation, whereas she is often pleading with pale propaganda. To be sure, methods of child delivery have altered with the advance of science; but again we say that science, that darling of the doctors, cannot shrink the nine months of child-formation. Brethren, we are beaten by the time element. The preacher and church, too busy to pray, are busier than the Lord would have them be. If we will give God time, He will give us timeless souls. If we will hide in our soul-impotence and call upon His name, He will bring forth our light as the noonday. The Church has advisers by the carload. But where are her agonizers? Churches, boasting an all-time high in attendance, might have to admit an all-time low in spiritual births. We can increase our churches without increasing the kingdom. (I know a family where all the children are adopted. Many of us preachers have more adoptions than births.) The enemy of multiplication is stagnation. When believers lacking births become burdened, and when soul-sterility sickens us, then we will pulsate with holy fear, and pray with holy fervor, and produce with holy fertility. At God's counter there are no "sale days," for the price of revival is ever the same—travail.

Surely this ruined race requires reviving. I am fully aware that there are those who in their sleepiness will swing back on the sovereignty of God and say, "When He moves, revival will come." That is only half-truth. Do you mean that the Lord is happy that eighty-three people per minute die without Christ? Have you fallen for the idea that the Lord is now willing that *many* should perish? Do you dare to say—what to me is little less than blasphemy—that when God decides to lift up His heel and scatter His enemies, then a mighty visitation will come? Never! Quote *part* of a text and you can make the Bible say anything. For instance, "God is able to do exceeding abundantly above all that we ask or think." Stop the verse there, and it means "God is *able* to do it, but as yet He is not bothered so to do." This verse, misquoted, leaves the lack of revival on the steps of God's throne. But finish the text . . . "able to do—according to the power *that worketh in us,*" and it means that the channel is blocked; it means God cannot get through to this age because of lack of power in the Church. So lack of revival is *our* fault.

Finney said: "God is one pent-up revival"; so we can have revival "according to the power that worketh in us," for we "shall receive power *after that the Holy Ghost is come upon* [us]." This is not power merely to do miracles, for *before* Pentecost they did miracles and cast out devils. Nor is it just power to organize, power to preach, power to translate the Scriptures, power to enter new territories for the Lord. All this is good. But have we Holy Ghost power—power that restricts the devil's power, pulls down strongholds, and obtains promises? Daring delinquents will be damned if they are not delivered from the devil's dominion. What has hell to fear other than a God-anointed, prayer-powered church?

Beloved, let us put away all trifling. Let us forget denominational issues. Let us "give ourselves *continually to prayer* and to the ministry of the Word," "for faith cometh by hearing." Shamed at the impotence of the Church, chagrined at the monopoly the devil holds, shall we not cry with tortured spirits (and mean it): *"Give me children, or else I die!"* Amen.

Christian men and women, self-renunciation is
the cardinal ethic of the Christian Church.
—Dr. Charles Inwood

"Now I leave off to speak any more to creatures, and turn
my speech to Thee, O Lord. Now I begin my intercourse
with God which shall never be broken off. Farewell, father
and mother, friends and relations! Farewell, meat and
drink! Farewell, the world and all delights! Farewell, sun,
moon, and stars! Welcome God and Father! Welcome
sweet Lord Jesus, Mediator of the New Covenant!
Welcome Blessed Spirit of Grace, God of all Consolation!
Welcome Glory! Welcome Eternal Life! Welcome Death!"
Dr. Matthew MacKail stood below the gallows, and as his
martyr cousin writhed in the tautened ropes, he clasped
the helpless jerking legs together and clung to them that
death might come the easier and sooner. And so, with
Christ was Hugh MacKail "with his sweet boyish smile."
"And that will be my welcome," he said;
"the Spirit and the Bride say, Come."
—The martyrdom of Hugh
MacKail, a Covenanter

CHAPTER SEVENTEEN

"The Filth of the World"

What is "the filth of this world"? (I Cor. 4:13). Is it the womb of evil of which the national syndicated crime is born? Is it the evil genius operating the international upheaval? Was it Babylon? Is it Rome? Is it sin? Has a tribe of evil spirits been located bearing this repulsive title? Is it V.D.?

A thousand guesses at this question might provide a thousand different answers with not one of them correct. The right answer is the very antithesis of our expectation. This *"filth of this world"* is neither of men nor of devils. It is not bad, but good—nay, not even good—but the very best. Neither is it material, but spiritual; neither is it of Satan, but of God. It is not only of the Church, but a saint. It is not only a saint, but the saintliest of saints, the Kohinoor of all gems. "We *apostles*," Paul says, *"are the filth of this world."* Then he adds insult to injury, heightens the infamy, and deepens the humiliation by adding "[and we apostles are] *the off-scouring of all things*" (I Cor. 4: 13).

Any man who has so assessed himself "filth of the earth" has no ambitions—and so has nothing to be jealous about. He has no reputation—and so has nothing to fight about. He has no possessions—and therefore nothing to worry about. He has no "rights"—so therefore he cannot suffer any wrongs. Blessed state! He is already dead—so no one can kill him. In such a state of mind and spirit, can we wonder that the apostles "turned the world upside down"? Let the ambitious saint ponder this apostolic attitude to the world. Let the popular, unscarred evangelist living in "Hollywood style" think upon his ways.

Who then hurt Paul far more than his one hundred and ninety-five stripes, his three stonings, and his triple shipwrecks could ever hurt him? The contentious, carnal, critical, Corinthian crowd. This Church was split by carnality—*and cash!* Some had rocketted to fame and become the merchant princes of the city. So Paul says, *"Ye* have reigned as kings without us." Ponder the glaring contrasts in I Cor. 4:8: "Ye are full, *ye* are rich, *ye* have reigned as kings without us." "We are fools; *we* are despised; *we* both hunger and thirst and are naked" (verse 10). The blessed compensation is in verse 9, "We [apostles] are made a spectacle unto the world, and to angels, and to men."

It was not hard for Paul to claim after all this that *he* was "less than the least." Then, Paul pointed all this truth against those whose faith had lost its focus. These Corinthians were full, but not free. (A man escaped from his cell is not free who still drags his chain.) Paul is not grieved that they have super-abundance and he nothing. He groans that their wealth has brought weakness of soul. They have comfort, but no cross; they are rich, but not reproached for Christ's sake. He does not say they are not Christ's, but that they are seeking a thornless path to heaven. He declares, "I would to God *ye* did reign, that *we* also might reign with you." If they were actually reigning, then Christ would have come, the millennium would have been there, and, Paul adds, *"We* would be reigning *with you."*

But who wants to be thus dishonored, despised, devalued? Such truth is revolutionary and upsetting to our corrupted Christian teaching. Can we *delight* in being esteemed fools? Is it *easy* to see our names cast about as an evil thing? Communism levels men down; Christ levels men up! True Christianity is far more revolutionary than Communism (though of course, bloodless). The bulldozers of socialism have tried to "push over" the hills of wealth and "fill in" the valleys of poverty. They thought that by education they could "make the crooked places straight"—by an act of parliament and a mere waving of the political wand, the millennium, so long delayed, could be brought in. But those changes in Russia have been merely a change of bosses with the underdog still the bottom dog. Today plenty of people are rich by making others poor, but Paul said he was "poor, *yet making many rich."* Thanks be unto God! the bag of Simon Magus still gets no attention from the Holy Ghost! If we have not yet been taught how to esteem "the mammon of unrighteousness," how shall we be entrusted with the "true riches"?

And so Paul, bankrupt materially and socially, was bracketed with the choice few who are listed "as the 'filth of the world.'" Certainly this helped him understand that, as filth, he would be trodden under foot by men. Even though he could answer the philosophers, Stoics, and Epicurians on Mars Hill, yet for Christ's sake he was willingly rated a "fool." To Jesus, the world's antagonism was fundamental and perpetual.

Brethren, is this our choice? What irks us more than to be *classified with unlearned and ignorant men?*—though an unlearned and ignorant man wrote "the Revelation," which still baffles the learned. We are suffering today from a plague of ministers who are more concerned that their *heads should be filled* than that their *hearts be fired*. If a preacher leans toward headiness, let him spend his years of schooling *before* he enters the pulpit. Once he gets there, he is in it for life. Added degrees will not matter, because twenty-four hours a day are not sufficient for him to bear the names of his flock before the Great Shepherd, or fulfill the parallel responsibility of preparing their soul-food. The fact, then, is that spiritual things are spiritually *(not psychologically)* discerned. Neither God nor His judgments have changed. By His prerogative, there are still things withheld from the prudent and "revealed unto babes." And babes, brethren, have no colossal intellects! The Church of this hour boasts an all-time high in the IQ of its ministry. But hold on a minute before we triumph in the flesh. We are also having an all-time low in spiritual births, for the devil shudders not, Brother Apollos, at your verbal Niagaras!

The line of demarcation from the world is distinct, deliberate, and discredited. Bunyan's pilgrims passing through Vanity Fair were a spectacle. In dress, speech, interest, and sense of values, they differed from the worldlings. Is this so in our lives today?

During the last war a British general said, "We must teach our men to hate, for what men hate they will fight." We have heard much (though not half enough) about perfect love; but we also need to know how to "be angry and sin not." The Spirit-filled believer will hate iniquity, injustice, and impurity; and he will militate against all of them. Because Paul hated the world, the world hated Paul. We, too, need this disposition of opposition.

Stanley wrote his "Darkest Africa," and General Booth his "Darkest England" amidst crushing opposition. The former saw the tall, impenetrable forest, with its lurking leopards, subtle snakes, and denizens of the darkness. Booth saw the English streets as God saw them—the lurking lust, the sewers of sin, the greed of gambling, the peril of prostitution—and he raised an army for God to fight them. Our front streets are now mission fields. Forget culture, for a well-mannered, nicely groomed and soft-spoken lady may be as far from God as the Mau Mau mother with her grass skirt. Our cities are alive with impurity. A Christian, dreaming before his television night by night, has a dead brain and a bankrupt soul. He would do better to persuade God to let him quit this world if he is so out of touch with this lax, loose, licentious age that blindness of the sinner no longer tears his soul. Every street is now a river of devilry, drink, divorce, darkness, and damnation. If you are taking a stand against all this, marvel not, brethren, that the world hate you. If ye were of the world, the world would love its own.

Paul declares in good round English, "The *world* is crucified unto me." Is this far beyond twentieth century Christians? Golgotha witnessed many crowds who came to see the humiliation of its malefactors. There was carnival at the Cross; there was mockery at misery. But who went the next morning to view the victims? The first callers were vultures—to peck out their eyes and strip their ribs; then dogs ate the limbs which hung from these hapless victims. Thus distorted, and decorated with his own entrails, the felon was a fright. Even so, to Paul, the crucified world was as unattractive as that!

Well might we, too, inwardly quake and with trembling lips repeat this phrase, *the world is crucified to me.* Only when we are thus "dead to the world and all its toys, its idle pomp and fading joys" can we feel the freedom that Paul knew. The plain fact is that we followers of Christ *respect* the world and its opinions and appreciations and qualifications. A modern critic says that we believers have *gold* for our god and *greed* for our creed. (Only those who are guilty will get mad at that quip!) On the other hand, in this year of grace, I do know some saints on both sides of the Atlantic who wear clothes that others have cast off, and so turn all their dollars and dimes (or pounds and pence) into grist for God's mill. With his strong emphasis on separation, one wonders that Paul ever got any converts at all.

This blessed man, to whom the world was crucified, was considered "mad." Moreover, Paul so presented his message that others sought his death, for their "craft was in danger!" Such blessed apostles, with their healthy, holy *disregard for the world* and its men, shame us.

> "They climbed the steep ascent to heaven
>   Through peril, toil and pain;
> O God, to us may grace be given
>   To follow in their train."

Soon it will be "Farewell mortality, welcome eternity." Here's wishing you, beloved believer, a year of sacrificial service for Him who was our sacrifice. May we, too, finish our course with *joy.*

Brethren, it is just so much humbug to be waiting for this,
night after night, month after month, if we ourselves are
not right with God. I must ask myself—"Is my heart pure?
Are my hands clean?"

—COMMENT FROM THE
HEBRIDES REVIVAL

My soul, ask what thou wilt,
Thou canst not be too bold;
Since His own blood for thee He spilt,
What else can He withhold?

—UNKNOWN

The place of prayer,
O fruitful place!
The Spirit hovers there;
For all embodiments of grace
Are from the womb of prayer.

—HAROLD BROKKE

Revival is no more a miracle than a crop of wheat. Revival
comes from heaven when heroic souls enter the conflict
determined to win or die—or if need be, to win and die!
"The kingdom of heaven suffereth violence, and
the violent take it by force."

—CHARLES G. FINNEY

God's cause is committed to men; God commits Himself to
men. Praying men are the vice-regents of God; they
do His work and carry out His plans.

—E. M. BOUNDS

Prayer is the sovereign remedy.

—ROBERT HALL

Prayer is the acid test of devotion.

—SAMUEL CHADWICK

CHAPTER EIGHTEEN

Prayer as Vast as God

God-gripped prophets of old had a sensitive awareness of the enormity and unpopularity of their task. By pleading their own inefficiency and inadequacy, these care-bowed men sought to escape the delivering of their burdened souls. Moses, for instance, sought to evade a nationwide commitment by pleading a stammering tongue. Yet note how God evaded his evasion by supplying a spokesman in Aaron. Jeremiah, too, reasoned that he was but a child. Yet in Jeremiah's case (as in Moses'), the human objection was not sustained. For men of divine selection were not sent to the council chambers of human wisdom—to get their personalities polished or their knowledge edged. But God somehow trapped His man and closeted him with Himself. If according to Oliver Wendell Holmes, a man's mind, stretched with a new idea, can never go back to its original dimensions, then what shall we say of a soul that has heard the whisper of the Eternal Voice? "The words that I [the Lord] speak unto you, they are spirit, and *they are life*" (John 6:63). Our preaching is much diseased today by borrowed thoughts from the brains of dead men rather than from the Lord. Books are good when they are our guides, but bad when they are our chains.

Just as in atomic energy, modern scientists have touched a new dimension of power, so the Church has to rediscover the unlimited power of the Holy Spirit. To smite the iniquity of this sin-soaked age and shatter the complacency of slumbering saints, something is really needed. Vital preaching and victorious living must "come out of" sustained watches in the prayer chamber. Some one says, "We must *pray* if we want to live a holy life!" Yes, but conversely, we must *live a holy life* if we want to pray. According to David, "Who shall ascend into the hill of the Lord? He that hath clean hands, and a pure heart" (Ps. 24:3-4).

The secret of praying is praying in secret. Books on prayer are good, but not enough. As books on cooking are good but hopeless unless there is food to work on, so with prayer. One can read a library of prayer books and not be one whit more powerful in prayer. We must learn to pray, and we must pray to learn to pray. While sitting in a chair reading the finest book in the world on physical health, one may waste away. So one may read about prayer, marvel at the endurance of Moses, or stagger at the weeping, groaning Jeremiah, and yet not be able to stammer the ABC's of intercessory prayer. As the bullet unspent bags no game, so the prayer-heart unburdened gathers no spoil.

"In God's name, I beseech you, let prayer nourish your soul as meals nourish your body!" said the faithful Fenelon. Henry Martyn spake thus: "My present deadness I attribute to want of sufficient time and tranquility for private devotion. Oh that I might be a man of prayer!" A writer of old said, "Much of our praying is like the boy who rings the door bell, but then runs away before the door is opened." Of this we are sure: The greatest undiscovered area in the resources of God is the place of prayer.

Who can tell the measure of God's powers? One might estimate the weight of the world, tell the size of the Celestial City, count the stars of heaven, measure the speed of lightning, and tell the time of the rising and setting of the sun— but you cannot estimate prayer power. *Prayer is as vast as God* because He is behind it. Prayer is as mighty as God, because He has committed Himself to answer it. God pity us that in this noblest of all employments for the tongue and for the spirit, we stammer so. If God does not illuminate us in the closet, we walk in darkness. At the judgment seat the most embarrassing thing the believer will face will be the smallness of his praying.

Here is a majestic passage from the venerated Chrysostom: "The *potency of prayer* hath subdued the strength of fire; it hath bridled the rage of lions, hushed anarchy to rest, extinguished wars, appeased the elements, expelled demons, burst the chains of death, expanded the gates of heaven, assuaged diseases, repelled frauds, rescued cities from destruction, stayed the sun in its course, and arrested the progress of the thunderbolt. Prayer is an all-sufficient panoply, a treasure undiminished, a mine which is never exhausted, a sky unobscured by clouds, a heaven unruffled by the storm. It is the root, the fountain, the mother, of a thousand blessings." Are Chrysostom's words mere rhetoric, to make a commonplace thing look superlative? The Bible knows nothing of such cunning.

Elijah was a man skilled in the art of prayer, who altered the course of nature, strangled the economy of a nation, prayed and fire fell, prayed and people fell, prayed and rain fell. We need rain, rain, rain! The churches are so parched that seed cannot germinate. Our altars are dry, with no hot tears of penitents. Oh for an Elijah! When Israel cried for water, a man smote a rock, and that flinty fortress became a womb out of which a life-giving stream was born. "Is anything too hard for the Lord?" God send us a man that can smite the rock!

Of this let us be sure, the prayer closet is not a place merely to hand to the Lord a list of urgent requests. Does "prayer change things"? Yes, but prayer *changes men.* Prayer not only took away the reproach of Hannah, but it changed her—changed her from a barren woman to a fruitful one, from mourning to rejoicing (I Sam. 1:10; and 2:1), yes, changed her "mourning into dancing" (Ps. 30:11). Perhaps we are praying that we might dance when we have never yet mourned. We choose the garment of praise while God says, (Isa. 61:3), *"unto them that mourn* [I give] the garment of praise for the spirit of heaviness." If we would reap, the same order is true, for "he that goeth forth and *weepeth,* bearing precious seed, shall doubtless come again with *rejoicing,* bringing his sheaves with him" (Ps. 126:6).

It took a *heartbroken, mourning* Moses to cry, "Oh, this people have sinned a great sin . . . Yet now, if thou wilt forgive their sin—; and if not, blot me, I pray thee, out of thy book which thou hast written" (Ex. 32:31-32)! It took a *burdened, pain-gripped* Paul to say, "I have great heaviness and continual sorrow in my heart. For I could wish that myself were accursed from Christ for my brethren, my kinsmen according to the flesh" (Rom. 9:2-3).

If John Knox had prayed, "Give me success!" we would never have heard of him; but he prayed a self-purged prayer—"Give me Scotland, or I die!"—and his prayer scored the pages of history. If David Livingstone had prayed that he might split Africa wide open, as proof of his indomitable spirit and skill with the sextant, his prayer would have died with the wind of the forest; but he prayed, "Lord, when will the wound of this world's sin be healed?" Livingstone lived in prayer, and literally died upon his knees in prayer.

For this sin-hungry age we need a *prayer-hungry* Church. We need to explore again the "exceeding great and precious promises of God." In "that great day," the fire of judgment is going to test the *sort,* not the *size* of the work we have done. That which is born in prayer will survive the test. Prayer does business with God. Prayer creates hunger for souls; hunger for souls creates prayer. The understanding soul prays; the praying soul gets understanding. To the soul who prays in self-owned weakness, the Lord gives His strength. Oh that we were men of like prayer as Elijah—a man subject to like passions as we are! Lord, let us pray!

On a tablet in a large church seating 1,000 people, this inscription was placed in memory of John Geddie: "When he landed in 1848 there were no Christians here; when he left in 1872 there were no heathen."

—MEMORIAL TO JOHN GEDDIE,
THE "FATHER" OF
PRESBYTERIAN MISSIONS IN
THE SOUTH SEAS

From the day of Pentecost, there has been not one great spiritual awakening in any land which has not begun in a union of prayer, though only among two or three; no such outward, upward movement has continued after such prayer meetings declined.

—DR. A. T. PIERSON

CHAPTER NINETEEN

As the Church Goes, So Goes the World

For this midnight hour, *incandescent* men are needed. On the day of Pentecost, the flame of the living God became the flame of the human heart to that glorious company. The Church *began* with these men in the "upper room" agonizing—and today is *ending* with men in the supper room organizing. The Church began in revival; we are ending in ritual. We started virile; we are ending sterile. Charter members of the Church were men of heat and no degrees; today many hold degrees, but have no heat! Ah, brethren, flame-hearted men are the crying need of the hour!

Men need to be a pillar of fire—God-guided men to lead a misguided people; passionate Pauls to stir timid Timothys; men of flame to outshine and outburn men of name! We need knights of prayer to lead nights of prayer. We need true *prophets* to warn of false *profits,* "for what shall it profit a man, if he shall gain the whole world and lose his own soul?" (Mark 8:36).

In this end time the rockaby-baby attitude of many conference preachers is a tragedy. The cry should be "Blow the trumpet in Zion, sanctify a fast, call a solemn assembly . . . ; let the priests, the ministers of the Lord, weep!" (Joel 2:15–17).

Compared to a heart that has known the fire of the Lord and allowed that fire to go out, the ice-clad peaks of the Alps are warm. Metal is molten only while the fire burns; remove the fire and the metal is solid. Even so, a human heart without the heat of heaven is an iceberg.

If the Spirit is absent, the preacher's study becomes a laboratory for dissecting doctrine and developing lifeless dogma. Teaching needs anointing; truth must be trenchant; and comfort must kindle.

Inspired men are desperately needed! Believers with Spirit-generated souls are indispensable to this degenerate generation. The gale of end-time iniquity will blow out a mere human flame and as a dry reed cracks in a storm, will snap fleshly sectarianism's feeble candle. At the moment a rushing mighty wind of false religion and lukewarm Christianity is lashing the world. Warned of false fire by fireless men, we too often settle for no fire at all!

Unable to detect what is flesh and what is Spirit, the religionists of the hour are heralding with banner headlines a new boom in spirituality. The good has again become the enemy of the best. (The wise will understand.) Be alarmed! The conflict gets stiffer! This is the night of blight and plight. God help the nations, ruined with *man-made* religion, cursed with *man-made* cults, and doomed with *man-made* doctrine! Was there ever such an evil hour? Reiterated effort is the price we have to pay for progress.

As the Church goes, so goes the world! If the watchmen sleep, the enemy takes the city! The preacher should give at least one day a week to prepare his sermons and yet another day to prepare the preacher to preach the prepared sermons. Inspiration is as mysterious as life, for both are God-given. Life begets life by its very nature. By the same token, inspired men inspire.

We need Joshuas to lead the Lord's people into the Promised Land of Spirit-empowered living. Like Israel, we have escaped Egypt and Pharaoh (which in our experience means the world and Satan), but failed at Kadesh-Barnea. What should be a stepping stone can become a stumbling block. What should be a gateway can become a goal. What could be a thoroughfare can become a terminal.

"Blind unbelief is sure to err and scan God's works in vain." Have we come out of the poverty of the world, but not yet entered into the Canaan of His riches?

Think of it! For forty years these chosen people had no miracles and no answers to prayer—nothing but deaths, droughts and darkness. And all because of unbelief. "The giants are too great for us!" was their cry (Num. 13:17–33). Today this is our cry. "Look at the might of this; measure, if you can, the strength of that!" Our reply should be, "Lord, I pray thee, open . . . eyes!" (II Kings 6:17). "Is the Lord's arm shortened that He cannot save" (Isa. 59:1)? Shall we but consider Him as the God of the past, the God of prophecy, but not the God of the present?

Peter's Pentecost sermon was as scorching as it was searching. Truth became alive. *"This is that which was spoken by the prophet Joel!"* (Acts 2:16). The inspired writer soon found that "this sword of the Lord" had a new edge so that the listeners were cut to the heart.

Men are ever saying that in these trying days people need comfort. Agreed—many do need comfort. The sick, the sad, and the suffering are in this bracket. However, let none fail to realize that to keep silent while a house is burning is criminal. He is no comforter who lets his neighbor sleep as he watches a criminal move to the door with a gun. (In this hour this is not overdrawing the picture of the peril.)

Before the men of straw of our day, who decry our blood-honoring, incarnation-believing, hell-fire evangelism, shall we wilt? To do this would reveal us as sawdust-Caesars. The legions of hell are great; but the legions of heaven are greater. The devil is mighty; God is Almighty. The stakes are high. The price and prize are great!

Some declare that in America Patrick Henry did more to pave the way for freedom and liberty than any other man in its history. Hear him, fired with passionate devotion for his people, as he speaks at the Virginia Convention, March 23, 1775: "Is life so dear or peace so sweet as to be purchased at the price of chains and slavery? Forbid it, Almighty God! I know not what course others may take. But as for me, give me liberty—or give me death!" Could Cato or Demosthenes surpass that oratorical gem? Can we translate it?

The fearful bondage and slavery that exists in the world today and threatens the rest of mankind is no fairy story! Though Communism may conquer the world (terrible and unimaginable as that might be), to the true child of God there is a greater horror—eternity for the unrepentant in an endless hell!

Perhaps we should get near Patrick Henry's language this way: "Is life's span so dear and are home comforts so engrossing as to be purchased with my unfaithfulness and dry-eyed prayerlessness? At the final bar of God, shall the perishing millions accuse me of materialism coated with a few Scripture verses?

"Forbid it, Almighty God! I know not what course others may take; but as for me, *GIVE ME REVIVAL* in my soul and in my church and in my nation—*or GIVE ME DEATH!*"

Whatsoever thou shalt bind on earth
shalt be bound in heaven.
—**Jesus**

Your adversary the devil, . . . resist, steadfast in the faith.
—**Peter**

Submit . . . to God. Resist the devil,
and he will flee from you.
—**James**

The more God's people reckon with the devil in their
praying, the more they will taste of the liberty of
the Spirit in dealing with the issues of life.
—**F. J. Perryman**

Lord, even demons are subject unto us in Thy name.
—**The Seventy**

O Hell, I see thee surging round;
But in my Lord a cleft I've found,
A solid, sure abiding place
From which my enemy I face,
As here with Thee at God's right hand,
I on Thy Calvary-Victory stand.
—**Unknown**

Should all the hosts of death
And powers of hell unknown
Put their most dreadful forms
Of rage or malice on,
I shall be safe; for Christ displays
SUPERIOR POWER and guardian grace.
—**Isaac Watts**

CHAPTER TWENTY

Known in Hell

Some preachers master their subjects; some subjects master the preacher; once in a while one meets a preacher who is both master of, and also mastered by his subject. The Apostle Paul, I am sure, was in that category.

Look at Paul in Ephesus (Acts 19). Seven men were attempting to use a religious formula over a Gadara-type of victim. But slinging theological terms or even Bible verses at devil-possessed men is as ineffective as snowballing Gibraltar in the hope of removing it. One man, demon-controlled, was an easy match for these seven silly sycophants. While the seven sons of Sceva fled into the streets, shirtless and shamed, the man filled with an unholy spirit increased his wardrobe with seven suits. And so, the seven wounded, fearful men told their own tale, for God turned their folly to the glory of Christ, so that His name was greatly feared and magnified. Spooky spiritists were converted; Jews and Greeks were saved; at a public bonfire, cult books to the value of fifty thousand pieces were burned. Surely that was making the wrath of man to praise Him! Listen, too, to the testimony of the demon, "Jesus I know, *AND PAUL I KNOW,* but who are ye?" (Acts 19:15). This is the highest praise that earth or hell affords—to be classified by the enemy as one with Jesus.

But how did Paul get that way? Why did demons know Paul? Had they beaten him too, or had he beaten them? Consider for a moment this man Paul. God and Paul were on intimate terms. Revelations were granted him. His servants were angels; at his finger tips were earthquakes. His Spirit-powered words shattered the fetters from the soul of a spirit-bound girl, whom men had snared as a fortuneteller. In Corinth, this mighty man Paul drained a part of the Slough of Despond, and there on the devil's doorstep established a church. Later, he snatched souls from under the nose of Caesar, right from Caesar's own household. And before kings Paul was at home, for he said, "I count myself happy King Agrippa!" Paul also stormed the intellectual capital of the world (Mars Hill) with resurrection truth and thereby routed their learned. While Paul lived, hell had no peace.

But what was Paul's armory? Where did he edge his blade? Paul more than once uses the phrase "I am persuaded," and therein lay his secret. Revealed truth held him like a vise. The Word, like the Lord, was immutable. Paul's anchor was cast in the depths of God's faithfulness. His battleaxe was the Word of the Lord; his strength was faith in that Word. So the Spirit alerted Paul to the coming strategy of the devil. Paul was not ignorant of his devices; therefore hell suffered. Even when men willed to assassinate Paul, an informer uncovered the plot, and men and demons were foiled.

Spirituality that saves men from hell and keeps men from vulgar sins is wonderful, but, I believe, elementary. When Paul went to the Cross, the miracle of conversion and regeneration took place; but later when he got *on* the Cross, the greater miracle of identification took place. That I believe is the masterly argument of the Apostle—to be dead *and* alive at the same time. "Ye *are* dead," Paul wrote the Galatians. Suppose we try this on ourselves first. Are we *dead?—dead* to blame or praise? *dead* to fashion and human opinion? *dead* so that we have no itch for recognition? *dead* so that we do not squirm if another gets praised for a thing that we engineered? Oh sweet, sublime, satisfying experience of the indwelling Christ by the Spirit! We, too, can sing with Wesley:

> *Dead* to the world and all its toys!
> Its idle pomp and fading joys!
> Jesus, my glory be!

Yes, Paul was *dead.* Then he added, "Nevertheless *I live,* yet not I." Christianity is the only religion in the world where a man's God comes and lives *inside* of him. Paul no longer wrestled with flesh (neither his own nor any other man's); he wrestled "against principalities, against powers, against the rulers of the darkness of this world." Does that shed any light on why this demon said, *"And Paul I know"?* Paul had been wrestling against the demon powers. (In these modern days, this art of binding and loosing that Paul knew is almost forgotten or else ignored.) On the last lap of his earthly pilgrimage, he declared, "I have fought a good fight." Demons could have said amen to that statement, for they suffered more from Paul than Paul suffered from them. Yes, Paul was *known in hell.*

Another anchor that held this soul undaunted was the wrath of a holy God upon sin. "Knowing the terror of the Lord he persuaded men" (II Cor. 5:11). Paul accounted men as *lost!* The other night I saw a picture thrown onto a screen; but in its blurred state it had no meaning. Then the operator's hand reached out and focused the slide. What a difference! Even so, we Christians need the Divine Hand to sharpen the picture of the lostness of men to our eternity-dimmed eyes. Because Paul loved His Lord with a perfect love, he also hated sin with a perfect hatred. Thus he saw men not only prodigals but also rebels—not just drifters from righteousness but conspirators in wickedness, who *must* be pardoned or punished. With the fierceness of Love's intensest blaze, he burned at the injustice of men subordinate to demon power. His watchword was "This one thing I do." He had no side issues, no books to sell. He had no ambitions—and so had nothing to be jealous about. He had no reputation—and so had nothing to fight about. He had no possessions—and therefore nothing to worry about. He had no "rights"—so therefore he could not suffer wrong. He was already broken—so no one could break him. He was "dead"—so none could kill him. He was less than the least—so who could humble him? He had suffered the loss of all things—so none could defraud him. Does this throw any light on why the demon said, "Paul I know"? Over this God-intoxicated man, hell suffered headaches.

Yet another anchor to the spirit of this saint was the efficacy of the blood of Jesus, and so the ability of Christ to save *fully*. "ALL have sinned and come short of the glory of God." Yes! But Christ is *able to save* to the uttermost ALL who come unto God by Him. Oh that the world might know the all-atoning Lamb! With Paul there was no limited atonement. Zealot he was and wanted to be. In the light of an eternal hell what were perishing things of clay? And in our present day what are honors among men? or what are the schemes of hell? Right now *men are LOST,* as well as after they die. Right now men are being swept into the vortex of a sewer of gross iniquity which ultimately will suck them down to an *ETERNAL HELL.* Is this true? Paul was convinced that it was. Then, "oh arm of the Lord, awake; put on strength"

(Isa. 51:9). "Make me Thy battleaxe and Thy weapons of war," I hear Paul say.

Another anchor for Paul was the blessed assurance that "to be absent from the body was to be present with the Lord" (II Cor. 5:8). No soul-sleep here! No interminable intermediate state! Out of life into life! At the thought of *eternity,* language is beggered and imagination staggered. Paul could "write off" stripes, imprisonments, fastings, weariness, and painfulness as *"light* affliction"—recompensed by the fact "so shall we ever be with the Lord." All the "shot and shell" of demons was wasted against Paul. Do you wonder now that one of them said, "And Paul I *know"?*

The final truth as an anchor to Paul's soul was *"WE MUST ALL APPEAR* before *the judgment seat of Christ"* (II Cor. 5:10). Living with eternity's values in view took the sting out of this oncoming test too. Living "right," here on earth (I do not mean just living righteously, but living after the pattern set in the Holy Word) takes care of the hereafter. Paul was so conformed to the image of the Son that he could say, "What things ye have both learned, and received, and heard, *and seen in me, do"* (Phil. 4:9). To copy copies is not normally safe, but it is safe to copy Paul, for he was *fully* surrendered, *wholly* sanctified, *completely* satisfied, yea, "complete in Christ."

Do you still wonder why a demon said, "And Paul I know"? I don't.

STUDY QUESTIONS

CHAPTER ONE

1. Why is prayer less attractive than many other types of ministry?
2. How are logic and zeal meaningless apart from "unction"?
3. In what way is prayer your primary means of obtaining resources to share God's truth?

CHAPTER TWO

4. Is it true that "Satan has little cause to fear most preaching"? Why or why not?
5. How does prayer changes what effort and words cannot?
6. What percentage of your prayer is done privately?

CHAPTER THREE

7. How many people do you know that are "so heavenly that they are of no earthly good," and how many who are

"so earthly they are of no heavenly good"? Based on your experience, which represents real trouble for the Church?

8. What are the problems with the idea of being content with having been saved and sanctified?
9. Are you willing to endure life-altering agony and suffering to receive God's vision and passion?

CHAPTER FOUR

10. Is it possible to have passion without prayer?
11. What must we be willing to give up in order to obtain the mind of Christ?
12. Would you prefer God to have partnership with you or to have ownership of you?

CHAPTER FIVE

13. Why is it true that contemporary evangelists—that is, all present-day disciples of Christ—have the same ability to reach a dying world as did those followers of the 1st century?
14. What does the term "useful brokenness" mean to you? Does it make sense—or do you see the two terms as mutually exclusive? Can you justify your answer when you hold it up to your specific life situations/choices?
15. What walls and dams are you prepared to open so that the waters of healing and growth might flow once again?

CHAPTER SIX

16. What things would change immediately in our world if the Church lived constantly "in the light of the judgment seat"?
17. With today's push toward "tolerance" and "pluralism" in mind, can we still teach that a person is only acceptable

to God through Jesus Christ? How will your answer affect your life?

18. What will you do if you are rejected or slandered because of your stand for truth?

CHAPTER SEVEN

19. How do humility and confession relate to Spirit anointing?

20. Consider Paul before Damascus—then consider him afterward, turning the world upside-down. What do you think he must have been willing to endure in the wilderness of Arabia?

21. Is it ever right to turn down a preaching opportunity because of issues related to money?

CHAPTER EIGHT

22. How are doubt and unbelief similar or different? In what ways can doubt damage faith?

23. Why is saying "Lord, You can do this" not an example of faith?

24. What parts of "self" do you recognize as hindering your union with Christ?

CHAPTER NINE

25. What would it take for modern-day prophets of God to be considered "mad" and "insane" by the world?

26. Is this "insane boldness" reserved for those with the gift of prophecy? Why or why not?

27. Are you willing to proclaim the truth even at the cost of your own life?

CHAPTER TEN

28. How can men be made of steel and yet be flexible enough for God to have His way?

29. Why is prayer a weapon rather than a defence?
30. Would Satan tremble if he considered your prayer life?

CHAPTER ELEVEN

31. How does sin lobotomize people's minds and hearts?
32. What is the difference between joy and "silliness"?
33. At what times in your daily life is your focus more on the things of this world than on eternity?

CHAPTER TWELVE

34. What is the problem with requesting the coming of the Holy Spirit while questioning His gifts?
35. Why is the Church in worse shape than the world?
36. What would you change immediately if you had six months to live?

CHAPTER THIRTEEN

37. What is the long-term difference between being alone and being lonely? Which of the two will remain, and which need not?
38. Why are we often more willing to pray for and contribute to people around the world than to help the people across the street?
39. If someone came to you and said, "I want to repent but I don't know how," what would you tell him/her?

CHAPTER FOURTEEN

40. How would the world today respond to the God-breathed preaching of Paul?
41. What decisions did Paul have to make in order that He might be fully broken for the glory of God?
42. What decisions are you willing to make so that you might be of service?

CHAPTER FIFTEEN

43. What marks people who are "branded by devotion"?
44. What was Paul's method for dealing with humiliation and pain?
45. To you, who are "the lost, the last, and the least"? What are you willing to sacrifice to reach them with Christ's love?

CHAPTER SIXTEEN

46. Is it possible to be too busy to pray? If so, is it possible to be praying too much to be busy?
47. Does our spiritual childlessness come more from sterility or from lack of union with God? Or both?
48. What limits do you place on how long you fervently pray for something that remains unfulfilled?

CHAPTER SEVENTEEN

49. Who today could rightly call themselves "the filth of the world"?
50. Is it true that if the world affirms or accepts us, it is proof we are not preaching the truth?
51. In what areas of life are you still in harmony with the world?

CHAPTER EIGHTEEN

52. What things stain the Church today and keep it from approaching God with a pure heart and clean hands?
53. In the realm of prayer, are we most concerned with the changing of God, the changing of circumstances, the changing of others, or the changing of ourselves?
54. If the final judgment were today, would you be confident in or ashamed of your prayer life?

CHAPTER NINETEEN

55. Have we, the Church, been so compromised that we can no longer recognize empty or counterfeit spirituality?

56. Are we insisting on remaining in the wilderness because the beauty and the challenge of Canaan are more than we wish to bear?

57. Do you proclaim peace and comfort when they are not present? Is it more important to you to be a peacemaker or a peacekeeper?

CHAPTER TWENTY

58. Is it possible for people today to have the same type of anointing as was given Paul?

59. How does the church live and minister today as though we believe everything the Bible says about eternity is true? In what ways do we fall short?

60. If you knew eternity was to face you in the next moment, what would you immediately change about your actions and interactions?

CLASSIC ANDREW MURRAY
Edited Especially for *Today's* Readers

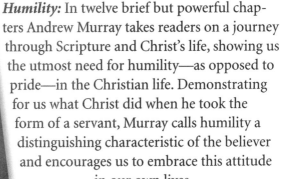

Humility: In twelve brief but powerful chapters Andrew Murray takes readers on a journey through Scripture and Christ's life, showing us the utmost need for humility—as opposed to pride—in the Christian life. Demonstrating for us what Christ did when he took the form of a servant, Murray calls humility a distinguishing characteristic of the believer and encourages us to embrace this attitude in our own lives.

The Ministry of Intercessory Prayer: Murray offers practical, biblical instruction in intercessory prayer as well as a 31-day course, "Pray Without Ceasing," at the end of the book. All of this is part of his simple but profound goal to change the world through intercession.

Abiding in Christ: Using the image of the vine and the branches to explain the concept of abiding in Christ, Murray offers a message as timely now as it was a century ago. He urges readers to yield themselves to Jesus in order to know "the full blessedness of abiding in Christ."

BETHANYHOUSE